Hugo's Simplified System

Chinese
Phrase Book

Hugo's Language Books Limited

Compiled by
Lexus Ltd
with
Huiqun Ye and Lesley Thirkell

*Facts and figures given in this book were
correct when printed. If you discover any
changes, please write to us.*

2nd impression 1993

Set in 9/9 Plantin Light by
Typesetters Ltd
Printed in Great Britain

CONTENTS

PREFACE

This Chinese Phrase Book has the same excellent pedigree as others in the Hugo series, having been compiled by experts to meet the general needs of tourists and business travellers, but it is – as you might expect – a little different. Arranged under the usual headings of 'Hotels', 'Shopping' and so forth, the Chinese words and phrases are printed in 'Pinyin', the standard system of romanization. Chinese characters are also shown, except in the *Things you'll hear* boxes. Although plenty of guidance is given regarding pronunciation (see pages 5-6), there are some tricky tones to master; if you feel unsure of yourself, simply point to the phrase you want to say.

Of course you will want to know what various signs and notices mean when they are written in Chinese characters; there are lists of common signs (pages 15-16) and road signs (page 31), as well as recognition boxes headed *Things you'll see* in most sections of the book. These cover words, signs, notices etc; the Chinese script is given alongside its Pinyin version and the English translation.

A 1200-line Mini-Dictionary will help you form additional phrases (or at least express the one word you need!), and the extensive Menu Reader will ease your way through complicated Chinese meals, which can be a world apart from those you find in your local take-away. Under the heading *Cross-cultural Notes* you will find guidance on aspects of the Chinese way of life – points of etiquette, good manners and customs. An understanding of such matters will greatly enhance your trip to China, and your hosts will appreciate all the effort you have made to respect their culture and to speak their language.

4

PRONUNCIATION

In this phrase book, Pinyin spelling is used. Pinyin is the usual method for writing Chinese in the Roman alphabet, but it is not a pronunciation system. The following consists of guidelines for pronouncing Pinyin:

CONSONANTS

c	like 'ts' in 'sets'
q	like 'ch' in 'China'
x	like the 's-y' sound in 'this year'
z	like 'ds' in 'beds'
zh	like 'j' in 'Jane'

VOWELS AND VOWEL COMBINATIONS

a	as in 'father'
ai	as in 'Shanghai'
ei	as in 'Beijing' or 'eight'
i	as in 'Maria' except in the following combinations: ci, chi, ri, si, shi, zi, zhi when it is pronounced as in 'sir'
ia	as 'ya' in 'yard'
ian	pronounced 'yen'
iang	pronounced 'yahng'
ie	pronounced as Old English 'yea'
iu	as 'yo' in 'yoke'
o	as in 'for'
ou	as in 'though'
u	as in 'too' (but in some instances as ü below)
ui	pronounced 'way'
uo	pronounced 'war'
ü	as in 'few' (also as in the German word 'über' or the French word 'du')

TONES

Chinese is a tonal language and has four tones. That means sounds can be pronounced with four different types of intonation. The first tone is flat and continuous as if briefly holding the same musical note. The second is a rising tone similar to the intonation of a question, for example 'Why?'. The third tone falls then rises resembling a note of surprise as in 'What!'. The fourth is a falling tone like the tone of an emphatic 'No!' in English.

First ¯ Second ´ Third ˇ Fourth `

Each Chinese word has its own written character and a fixed tone in spoken Chinese. Mistakes can lead to a degree of confusion in spoken (though not in written) Chinese as tones can affect meaning:

> mǎi is 'to buy' and mài is 'to sell'
> mǎ is 'horse' and mā is 'mother'
> táng is 'sugar' and tāng is 'soup'

CROSS-CULTURAL NOTES

* meeting Chinese

Visitors to China are usually surprised by the considerable attention paid to foreigners. Although this can be very intimidating, it is just curiosity, particularly if the foreigner has blond hair, a beard or is tall. Trying to communicate with the 'audience', or even trying to take their photo can help disperse the crowd.

The equivalent in Chinese to 'Mr' and 'Mrs'is rarely used, and so it can be quite hard to know how to address people, particularly in a formal situation. Generally, a person's surname is followed by their job title. So *Mr* Li Hong (surname first), a teacher, would be called Li Lǎoshi. Among friends, people are often called young (*xiǎo*) or old (*lǎo*), depending on their relationship to the speaker. So, a younger friend might be called Xiǎo Li, and an older or more respected person, Lǎo Li. If in doubt, use the whole name.

Chinese people are very hospitable and sometimes invite foreigners to visit, eat in or stay in their homes. If invited, it is polite to accept, but be aware that it is technically illegal for foreigners to stay in Chinese people's homes without specific police permission. If you stay the night, you could cause your host a great deal of trouble.

The Chinese find expensive gifts embarrassing but it would be acceptable to offer such things as foreign postage stamps or cassettes of Western music.

* conversation

Most young people have studied English, although it is sometimes easier to communicate by writing things down because students rarely learn to speak or listen to English at school. Many people seize every opportunity to practise their English on a native speaker. This can become irritating but can also help you to meet some interesting people. When chatting to Chinese people, topics such as family, marital status, income, life at home and opinions of China are popular. Do not insist on discussing politics, particularly in public places, unless all the people you are with seem happy to do so.

* dress

Scanty clothing is generally frowned upon, particularly in the countryside, when worn by either foreigners or young Chinese.

* personal conduct and manners

Overt displays of affection, such as kissing in public, can be regarded as offensive. Chinese table manners are fairly lax, but gesticulating with chopsticks should be avoided.

* toilets

Although tourist hotels provide Western-style toilets, most other toilets tend to be fairly primitive and without seats. Many Chinese homes do not have a private toilet, so public toilets are very common and easy to find. It is advisable to carry a supply of toilet paper with you at all times.

* photographs

Military and strategic sites, for example, bridges, harbours etc., must not be photographed. Otherwise, photographs can be taken freely, but you should be tactful, as many old people find being photographed very distressing.

* travel

It is necessary to be patient and easy-going while travelling in China, as conditions can be very stressful. It is important to realise that more can be achieved by being calm and friendly. Buying tickets can be a very time-consuming business. Occasionally, Chinese people will offer to help with your problem.

* restricted areas

Certain areas of China are closed to foreigners. Going to these areas without a travel permit from the police can result in deportation. The number of 'open' areas has increased dramatically over the years and now most areas of interest to foreign tourists are open. Generally, areas are closed because of poverty, a lack of facilities deemed suitable for foreigners, or for military reasons.

* religion

Officially there is religious freedom in China. There are large numbers of Muslims, and Xinjiang and Ningxia are Autonomous Islamic Regions. Similarly, Tibet and its surrounding areas are strongly Tibetan Buddhist. Monks usually welcome foreigners who wish to visit temples. Throughout China there are also small pockets of Christians, both Catholic and Protestant. However, in most of China, religion is not an important facet of life.

USEFUL EVERYDAY PHRASES

Yes/no
In Chinese there is no single word for 'yes' or 'no'. Instead, the verb from the question is repeated as the affirmative 'yes'. For 'no', the negative word *'bù'* is used before the verb from the question. For example: 'do you want ...?' (*nǐ yào bú yào ...?*) – 'yes' = *'yào'*, 'no' = *'bú yào'*; 'are you ...?' (*nǐ shì bú shì*) – 'yes' = *'shì'*, 'no' = *'bú shì'*. The only exception is with the verb 'to have'. Instead of *'bù'*, use the word *'méi'*. For example: 'do you have ...?' (*nǐ yǒu méi yǒu?*) – 'yes' = *'yǒu'*, 'no' = *'méi yǒu'*.

Thank you
Xièxie
谢谢

No thank you
Búyaò, xièxie
不要，谢谢

Please
Qǐng
请

Please *(accepting)*
Yào
要

I don't understand
Wǒ bù dǒng
我不懂

Do you speak English?
Nǐ shuō Yīngyǔ ma?
你说英语吗？

I can't speak Chinese
Wǒ búhuì shuō Hànyǔ
我不会说汉语

I don't know
Wǒ bù zhīdào
我不知道

Please speak more slowly
Qǐng shuō màn yí xie
请说慢一些

Please write it down for me
Qǐng nǐ géi wó xiěyíxià
请你给我写一下

My name is ...
Wǒ jiào ...
我叫…

How do you do, pleased to meet you
Ní hǎo, hěn gāoxìng rènshi nǐ
你好，很高兴认识你

Good morning/good afternoon/good evening
Ní hǎo
你好

Good night
Wǎn ān
晚安

Goodbye
Zàijiàn
再见

USEFUL EVERYDAY PHRASES

How are you?
Ní hǎo ma?
你好吗？

Excuse me please (*to get attention*)
Láojià
劳驾

Sorry!
Duìbùqǐ
对不起

I'm really sorry
Zhēn duìbuqǐ
真对不起

Can you help me?
Nǐ néng bù néng bāngzhù wǒ?
你能不能帮助我？

Can you tell me ...?
Nǐ néng bù néng gàosù wǒ ...?
你能不能告诉我…？

Can I have ...?
Wǒ néng bù néng yào ...?
我能不能要…？

I would like ...
Wó xiǎng yào ...
我想要…

Is there ... here?
Zhèlǐ yǒu méi yǒu ...?
这里有沒有…？

Where can I get ...?
Nálǐ yǒu ...?
哪里有…？

How much is it?
Duōshǎo qián?
多少钱？

What time is it?
Xiànzài jí diǎn zhōng?
现在几点钟？

I must go now
Wǒ déi zǒu le
我得走了

I've lost my way
Wǒ mí lù le
我迷路了

Cheers! *(toast)*
Gānbēi!
干杯！

Do you take credit cards?
Kéyǐ yòng xìnyòngkǎ ma?
可以用信用卡吗？

Where is the toilet?
Cèsuǒ zài nálǐ?
厕所在哪里？

Go away!
Zǒu kāi!
走开！

USEFUL EVERYDAY PHRASES

Excellent!
Hǎo jí le!
好极了！

THINGS YOU'LL HEAR

Méiyǒu
We don't have any

Bùxíng
It's not possible

Dāngxīn
Look out!

Bú kèqì
You're welcome

Huānyíng
Welcome

Xièxie
Thanks

Duìbuqǐ
Pardon

Ní hǎo, hěn gāoxìng rènshi nǐ
How do you do, nice to meet you

Zàijiàn
Goodbye

Méi guānxì
It doesn't matter

→

Láojià
Excuse me

Wǒ bù dǒng
I don't understand

Wǒ bù zhīdào
I don't know

Zěnme le?
What's the matter?

Yào bú yào?
Do you want it?

THINGS YOU'LL SEE

办公室	bàngōngshì	office
不营业	bù yíngyè	not open for business
厕所	cèsuǒ	toilet
出口	chūkǒu	way out
电梯	diàntī	lift
付款台	fùkuǎn tái	pay here
坏了	huàile	out of order
静	jìng	silence (*in hospitals, libraries*)
禁止拍照	jìnzhǐ pāizhào	no photographs!
军事要地，请勿靠近	jūnshì yàodì, qǐng wù kàojìn!	military zone, keep out! →

15

USEFUL EVERYDAY PHRASES

开	kāi	open
开放时间	kāifàng shíjiān	opening times
拉	lā	pull
男	nán	gentlemen
女	nǔ	ladies
票	piào	tickets
入口	rùkǒu	way in
上	shàng	up
收款台	shōukuǎn tái	till (*check out*)
太平门	tàipíngmén	emergency exit
推	tuī	push
外宾止步	wàibīn zhǐbù	no foreigners allowed
危险	wēixiǎn!	danger!
下	xià	down
营业时间	yíngyè shíjiān	business hours
游人止步	yóurén zhǐbù	private

DAYS, MONTHS, SEASONS

Sunday	xīngqītiān	星期天
Monday	xīngqīyī	星期一
Tuesday	xīngqīèr	星期二
Wednesday	xīngqīsān	星期三
Thursday	xīngqīsì	星期四
Friday	xīngqīwǔ	星期五
Saturday	xīngqīliù	星期六
January	yīyuè	一月
February	èryuè	二月
March	sānyuè	三月
April	sìyuè	四月
May	wǔyuè	五月
June	liùyuè	六月
July	qīyuè	七月
August	bāyuè	八月
September	jiǔyuè	九月
October	shíyuè	十月
November	shíyīyuè	十一月
December	shí'èryuè	十二月
Spring	chūntiān	春天
Summer	xiàtiān	夏天
Autumn	qiūtiān	秋天
Winter	dōngtiān	冬天

Christmas	shèngdàn jié	圣诞节
New Year	yuándàn	元旦
Chinese New Year	chūn jié	春节
National Day	guóqìng jié	国庆节
The Mid-Autumn Festival	zhōngqiū jié	中秋节
Chinese New Year's Eve	dànián sānshí	大年三十

NUMBERS

0	líng	零	**10**	shí	十	
1	yī	一	**11**	shíyī	十一	
2	èr/liǎng	二／两	**12**	shí'èr	十二	
3	sān	三	**13**	shísān	十三	
4	sì	四	**14**	shísì	十四	
5	wǔ	五	**15**	shíwǔ	十五	
6	liù	六	**16**	shíliù	十六	
7	qī	七	**17**	shíqī	十七	
8	bā	八	**18**	shíbā	十八	
9	jiǔ	九	**19**	shíjiǔ	十九	

20	èrshí	二十
21	èrshíyī	二十一
22	èrshí'èr	二十二
30	sānshí	三十
31	sānshíyī	三十一
32	sānshí'èr	三十二
40	sìshí	四十
50	wǔshí	五十
60	liùshí	六十
70	qīshí	七十

NUMBERS

80 bāshí	八十	110 yìbǎi yìshí	一百一十
90 jiǔshí	九十	111 yìbǎi shíyī	一百十一
100 yìbǎi	一百	120 yìbǎi èrshí	一百二十
101 yìbǎi líng yī	一百零一	200 èrbǎi	二百
		300 sānbǎi	三百

1000 yìqiān	一千
10,000 yíwàn	一万
20,000 èrwàn	二万
100,000 shíwàn	十万
1,000,000 yī bǎiwàn	一百万
10,000,000 yī qiānwàn	一千万
100,000,000 yí yì	一亿

Note that Chinese has a unit for 10,000, a *'wàn'*; for example: 10,000 is *'yí wàn'* (literally one x 10,000) and 100,000 is *'shí wàn'* (literally 10 x 10,000). Note also that there are two words for '2'. In a counting sequence (1-2-3-4) use *'èr'*. But when referring to two objects, two people etc use *'liǎng'*. So for example, 'I want two tickets' is *'wǒ yào liǎng zhāng piào'*.

MEASURE WORDS

Chinese uses counting or measure words between the number and the noun. For example, 'one ticket' is *'yì zhāng piào'* where *'zhāng'* is the measure word for 'ticket'; 'two horses' is *'liǎng pí mǎ'* where *'pí'* is the measure word for 'horses'. There are a large number of measure words, the use of which depends on the type of object being talked about. A general measure word is *'gè'* which, while not always technically correct, can be used in most contexts.

TIME

today	jīntiān	今天
yesterday	zuótiān	昨天
tomorrow	míngtiān	明天
the day before yesterday	qiántiān	前天
the day after tomorrow	hòutiān	后天
this week	zhège xīngqī	这个星期
last week	shàngge xīngqī	上个星期
next week	xiàge xīngqī	下个星期
this morning	jīntiān shàngwǔ	今天上午
this afternoon	jīntiān xiàwǔ	今天下午
this evening	jīntiān wǎnshàng	今天晚上
tonight	jīnwǎn	今晚
yesterday afternoon	zuótiān xiàwǔ	昨天下午
last night	zuótiān wǎnshàng	昨天晚上
fortnight	liǎngge xīngqī	两个星期
six months	bànnián	半年
tomorrow morning	míngtiān shàngwǔ	明天上午
tomorrow night	míngtiān wǎnshàng	明天晚上
in three days	sāntiān hòu	三天后
three days ago	sāntiān qián	三天前
late	wǎn	晚

early	zǎo	早
soon	kuài	快
later on	yǐhòu	以后
at the moment	xiànzài	现在
second	miǎo	秒
minute	fēn	分
one minute	yì fēnzhōng	一分钟
two minutes	liǎng fēnzhōng	两分钟
quarter of an hour	yí kèzhōng	一刻钟
half an hour	bàn xiǎoshí	半小时
three quarters of an hour	sān kèzhōng	三刻钟
hour	xiǎoshí	小时
that day	nà tiān	那天
every day	měitiān	每天
all day	zhěngtiān	整天
the next day	dì'èrtiān	第二天

TELLING THE TIME

In Chinese, '*diǎn zhōng*' corresponds to the word 'o'clock' and follows the number. To show time after the hour, simply add the number of minutes, without '*zhōng*': 'three twenty' is '*sān diǎn èr shí*'.

However, up to ten past the hour, the word for 'minute', '*fēn*', should also be added. So for example 'ten past three' is '*sān diǎn shí fēn*'. 'Past' is '*guò*', 'quarter' is '*yíkè*'; so 'quarter past three' is '*sāndiǎnguò yíkè*'. 'To' is '*chà*'; so 'quarter to three' is '*sāndiǎn chà yíkè*'. 'Half' is '*bàn*' so 'half past three' is '*sān diǎn bàn*'.

Timetables use the 24 hour clock, written in Arabic numerals.

Note that for 'two' the word *'liǎng'* is used when telling the time, not *'èr'*.

am	shàngwǔ
pm	xiàwǔ
one o'clock	yī diǎnzhōng
ten past one	yīdiǎn shífēn
quarter past one	yīdiǎn guò yíkè
half past one	yīdiǎn bàn
twenty to two	liángdiǎn chà èrshífēn
quarter to two	liángdiǎn chà yíkè
two o'clock	liángdiǎnzhōng
13.00	xiàwǔ yīdiǎn zhōng
16.30	xiàwǔ sìdiǎn bàn
at half past five	wúdiǎn bàn
at seven o'clock	qī diǎnzhōng
noon	zhōngwǔ
midnight	bànyè

For dates add *'hào'* to the number, for example:

11th	shíyīhào

HOTELS

In China, there are many different types of hotel, ranging from international joint venture hotels to very basic youth hostel-like accommodation. International standard luxury hotels, often known as *'bīnguǎn'*, charge international rates and are almost exclusively for foreign visitors. There are also many high-quality nationally-owned hotels, often called *'fàndiàn'*, which provide a good or high degree of comfort and service. These hotels admit both foreign and Chinese guests. The more basic hotels, usually called *'lǚguǎn'*, offer very cheap accommodation, but they will not allow foreigners to stay without a great deal of persuasion. Only certain hotels have permission to admit foreigners, and in many areas, this law is strictly enforced.

Chinese hotels rarely provide rooms with a double bed, so you would have to make a point of asking for this. Expect to find rooms with twin-beds or, in the lower-grade hotels, rooms with 4, 6 and 8 beds or even dormitories. Meals are rarely included in the price of a room, although most hotels have a restaurant, serving at specific times only. Bathroom and shower facilities are rarely en suite, and you will usually find that they are situated along the corridor. Foreigners nearly always have to pay their hotel bill in FEC.

USEFUL WORDS AND PHRASES

balcony	yángtái	阳台
bathroom	yùshì	浴室
bed	chuáng	床
bedroom	wòshì	卧室
bill	zhàngdān	账单
breakfast	zǎofàn	早饭
dining room	cāntīng	餐厅

dinner	wǎncān	晚餐
dormitory	tǒng pù fángjiān	统铺房间
dormitory bed	tǒng pù	统铺
double bed	shuāngrén chuáng	双人床
double room	shuāngrén fángjiān	双人房间
foyer	xiūxītīng	休息厅
hotel	fàndiàn	饭店
key	yàoshi	钥匙
lift	diàntī	电梯
lounge	xiūxīshì	休息室
lunch	wǔfàn	午饭
manager	jīnglǐ	经理
reception	fúwùtái	服务台
receptionist	fúwùyuán	服务员
restaurant	cāntīng	餐厅
room	fángjiān	房间
room service	sòng fàn fúwù	送饭服务
shower	línyù	淋浴
single room	dānrén fángjiān	单人房间
toilet	cèsuǒ	厕所
twin room	shuāngrén fángjiān	双人房间

Have you any vacancies?
Hái yǒu kōng fángjiān ma?
还有空房间吗？

I have a reservation
Wǒ yǐjing yùdìngle fángjiān
我已经预订了房间

I'd like a single/twin room
Wó xiǎngyào yígè dānrén/shuāngrén fángjiān
我想要一个单人／双人房间

I'd like a room with a double bed
Wó xiǎngyào yígè yǒu shuāngrén chuáng de fángjiān
我想要一个有双人床的房间

I'd like a bed in the dormitory
Wó xiǎngyào yígè tǒng pù
我想要一个统铺

I'd like a room with a bathroom/balcony
Wó xiǎngyào yígè dài yùshì/yángtái de fángjiān
我想要一个带浴室／阳台的房间

I'd like a room for one night/three nights
Wó xiǎngyào yígè fángjiān zhù yíyè/sānyè
我想要一个房间住一夜／三夜

What is the charge per night?
Duōshǎo qián yíyè?
多少钱一夜？

I don't know yet how long I'll stay
Wǒ hái bù zhīdào wǒ yào dāi duōjiǔ
我还不知道我要呆多久

When is breakfast/dinner?
Jídiǎn chī zǎofàn/wǎnfàn?
几点吃早饭／晚饭？

Would you have my luggage brought up?
Qǐng sòng yíxià xínglǐ, hǎoma?
请送一下行李，好吗？

Please call me at ... o'clock
Qǐng zài ... diǎn jiào wǒ yíxià
请在…点叫我一下

Can I have breakfast in my room?
Wǒ kéyǐ zài zìjǐ fángjiānlǐ yòng zǎocān ma?
我可以在自己房间里用早餐吗？

I'll be back at ... o'clock
Wǒ ... diǎn huílái
我…点回来

My room number is ...
Wǒde fángjiān hàomǎ shì ...
我的房间号码是…

I'm leaving tomorrow
Wǒ míngtiān líkāi zhèr
我明天离开这儿

Can I have the bill please?
Qǐng géi wǒ jiéyíxià zhàng, hǎoma?
请给我结一下账，好吗？

I'll pay by credit card
Wó xiǎng yòng xìnyòngkǎ fùzhàng
我想用信用卡付账

Can you get me a taxi?
Nǐ néng bāng wǒ jiào liàng chūzūchē ma?
你能帮我叫辆出租车吗？

Can you recommend another hotel?
Nǐ néng géi wǒ tuījiàn qítā fàndiàn ma?
你能给我推荐其它饭店吗？

27

THINGS YOU'LL SEE

安全门	ānquánmén	emergency exit
餐厅	cāntīng	restaurant
厕所	cèsuǒ	toilet
电梯	diàntī	lift
服务台	fúwùtái	reception
客满	kèmǎn	no vacancies
拉	lā	pull
淋浴	línyù	shower
盆浴	pényù	bath
推	tuī	push
洗手间	xíshǒujiān	washroom
一层	yīcéng	ground floor

THINGS YOU'LL HEAR

Duìbuqǐ, kèmǎnle
I'm sorry, we're full

Méiyǒu dānrén fángjiānle
There are no single rooms left

Zhù jǐyè?
For how many nights?

Qǐng yùxiān fùkuǎn
Please pay in advance

MOTORING

It is extremely unusual for a foreigner to be allowed to drive a car in China, even with an international licence. Although it may be possible to hire a car (but only in Beijing and Guangzhou), considerable restrictions will apply. The most common way to travel by car is to hire one complete with driver. Many hotels have taxis for this purpose.

Traffic rules, particularly outside large cities, tend to be very lax. Drive on the right, overtake on the left. At traffic lights, traffic turning right should drive on – there is no need to stop for the lights. Traffic coming onto a roundabout has priority. Speed limits vary from area to area, and are rarely adhered to. In towns, the limit is generally as low as 30km/hr. Out of towns, the limit is approximately 60km/hr. There are no seatbelts in vehicles in China.

China does not have Western-style petrol stations. Instead, petrol is bought from government-controlled outlets with officially-issued ration coupons. It is very difficult for an individual to purchase petrol, so before hiring any kind of vehicle, it is vital to ensure you have enough fuel for your journey.

USEFUL WORDS AND PHRASES

breakdown gùzhàng   故障

car xiǎoqìchē   小汽车

to drive kāichē   开车

garage (*for repairs*) qìchē   汽车修理厂
  xiūlíchǎng

      (*for petrol*) jiāyóuzhàn   加油站

licence jiàshǐ zhízhào   驾驶执照

petrol qìyóu   汽油

van péngchē   篷车

I'd like some petrol/oil/water
Wó xiǎng yào qìyóu/jīyóu/shǔi
我想要汽油／机油／水

Will you drive us around today?
Jīntiān nǐ néng kāichē dài wǒmen chūqù ma?
今天你能开车带我们出去吗？

I'd like to hire a car
Wó xiǎng yào zū yíliàng chē
我想要租一辆车

How much will it cost?
Yào duōshǎo qián?
要多少钱？

How much is it per kilometre?
Měi gōnglǐ yào duōshǎo qián?
每公里要多少钱？

Please stop here
Qǐng zài zhèlǐ tíng yíxià
请在这里停一下

Please wait here for ... minutes
Qǐng zài zhèlǐ děng ... fēnzhōng
请在这里等…分钟

Please drive to ...
Qíng bǎ chē kāi dào ...
请把车开到…

SOME COMMON ROAD SIGNS

此路不通	cǐ lù bù tōng	no through road
单行线	dānxíngxiàn	one-way street
禁止超车	jìnzhǐ chāo chē	no overtaking
禁止鸣笛	jìnzhǐ míngdí	do not sound vehicle horn
禁止停车	jìnzhǐ tíng chē	no parking
禁止通行	jìnzhǐ tōngxíng	road closed
慢	màn	slow
前方施工	qiánfāng shīgōng	roadworks
让	ràng	give way
人行道	rénxíngdào	pedestrians
人行横道	rénxínghéngdào	pedestrian crossing
危险	wēixiǎn	danger
小心	xiǎoxīn	caution
注意行人	zhùyì xíngrén	beware of pedestrians

THINGS YOU'LL SEE

柴油	cháiyóu	diesel
汽油	qìyóu	petrol
加油站	jiāyóuzhàn	petrol station
车库	chēkù	garage

THINGS YOU'LL HEAR

zhào zhí zǒu
straight on

zài zuǒ biān
on the left

xiàng zuó guǎi
turn left

zài yòu biān
on the right

xiàng yòu guǎi
turn right

kào yòu dì yi ge guǎi wān
first on the right

kào zuǒ dì èr ge guǎi wān
second on the left

guòle ...
past the ...

Kéyǐ kàn yíxià nǐde zhízhào ma?
May I see your licence?

RAIL TRAVEL

The Chinese train network is extensive and punctual, covering huge distances with little delay. However, the system is hopelessly overloaded and this means that it is very difficult to buy tickets.

First class, 'soft sleeper' (ruǎn wò), is usually reserved for VIPs and foreigners, and consists of four-bed compartments. These are very luxurious, and each carriage has its own washroom and toilets. 'Hard sleeper' (yìng wò) is second class with sixty berths to a carriage. There is a long open corridor down one side of the carriage and berths are grouped in sections of two tiers of three. This is the most popular way to travel and consequently the hardest type of ticket to buy. Third class, 'hard seat' (yìng zuò), can be likened to travelling in a sardine tin. Passengers boarding mid-route are usually unable to buy a seat ticket, so they stand throughout their journey and the carriage can become extremely overcrowded. Hard seat tickets are, however, very cheap and are the easiest tickets to buy.

There are no return tickets in China and tickets can only be bought at the point of departure not more than three days in advance. To avoid the long queues at the railway stations, you should try to buy your ticket through CITS, although bookings must be made at least five days in advance and paid for in FEC, whereas most stations will accept RMB (see BANKS AND MONEY).

Once on the train, there is a restaurant car which serves three meals a day and a trolley service. In both cases, meal tickets should be bought in advance from a train employee who passes through the train. Food is also sold on every platform throughout the journey. Each train has at least one water boiler which supplies the only water suitable for drinking on the train.

It is often possible, with a lot of persistence, to upgrade a ticket once on the train. Each train has an office for this purpose but you need to be quite determined to do this – being pleasant and friendly is usually far more effective than losing your temper!

USEFUL WORDS AND PHRASES

attendant lièchēyuán 列车员

boiled water kāishuǐ 开水

booking office shòupiàochù 售票处

connection zhōngzhuǎn 中转

dining car cānchē 餐车

emergency applied brake jǐnjí zhìdòngzhá 紧急制动闸

entrance rùkǒu 入口

exit chūkǒu 出口

first class (*soft sleeper*) ruǎnwò 软卧

get in shàngchē 上车

get out xiàchē 下车

guard lièchēzhǎng 列车长

left luggage office xínglǐ jìcún chù 行李寄存处

lost property shīwù zhāolǐng 失物招领

luggage rack xínglǐ jià 行李架

platform zhàntái 站台

platform ticket zhàntái piào 站台票

railway tiělù 铁路

seat zuòwèi 座位

second class (*hard sleeper*) yìngwò 硬卧

single ticket dānchéng piào 单程票

soft seat ruǎnzuò 软座

station	huǒchēzhàn	火车站
station master	zhànzhǎng	站长
third class *(hard seat)*	yìngzuò	硬座
ticket	chēpiào	车票
timetable	lièchē shíkè biǎo	列车时刻表
train	huǒchē	火车
waiting room	hòuchēshì	候车室

When does the train for ... leave?
Qù ... de huǒchē jídiǎn chūfā?
去…的火车几点出发？

When is the next train to ...?
Qù ... de xiàyítàng chē shì jídiǎn?
去…的下一趟车是几点？

When is the first train to ...?
Qù ... de tóubānchē shì jídiǎn?
去…的头班车是几点？

When is the last train to ...?
Qù ... de mòbānchē shì jídiǎn?
去…的末班车是几点？

How much is the fare to ...?
Qù ... de chēpiào duōshǎo qián?
去…的车票多少钱？

Do I have to change?
Wǒ yào huàn chē ma?
我要换车吗？

I want to change my ticket to a hard sleeper/soft sleeper
Wó xiǎngyaò bá wǒde piào huànchéng yìngwò/ruǎnwò
我想要把我的票换成硬卧／软卧

I want to buy a hard seat ticket
Wó xiáng mǎi yìzhāng yìngzuò piào
我想买一张硬座票

How long does it take to get to …?
Dào … qù yào duōcháng shíjiān?
到…去要多长时间？

A ticket to … please
Qíng mǎi yìzhāng qù … de piào
请买一张去…的票

Is this the right train for …?
Zhè shì qù … de huǒchē ma?
这是去…的火车吗？

Is this the right platform for the … train?
Qù … shì zhège zhàntái shàngchē ma?
去…是这个站台上车吗？

Which platform for the … train?
Qù … shì jǐ hào zhàntái?
去…是几号站台？

Is this seat taken?
Zhège wèizi yǒurén ma?
这个位子有人吗？

This seat is taken
Zhège wèizi yǐjīng yǒurén le
这个位子已经有人了

Can I change to the bottom/middle/top bunk?

Wǒ néng bù néng huàn dào xiàpù/zhōngpù/shàngpù?

我能不能换到下铺／中铺／上铺？

Can I shut/open the curtains?

Wǒ kéyǐ lāshàng/lākāi chuānglián ma?

我可以拉上／拉开窗帘吗？

Where is the boiled water?

Kāishuǐ zài nálǐ?

开水在哪里？

Where is the toilet?

Cèsuǒ zài nálǐ?

厕所在哪里？

May I open/close the window?

Wǒ kéyǐ kāi/guān chuāng ma?

我可以开／关窗吗？

When do we arrive in ...?

Wǒmen shénme shíhòu dàodá ...?

我们什么时候到达…？

What station is this?

Zhè shì shénme zhàn?

这是什么站？

Do we stop at ...?

Wǒmen zài ... tíng ma?

我们在…停吗？

Would you keep an eye on my things for a moment?

Qǐng nǐ bāng wǒ kān yīhuir dōngxi, hǎo ma?

请你帮我看一会儿东西，好吗？

37

Is there a restaurant car on this train?
Zhè tàng chē shàng yǒu cānchē ma?
这趟车上有餐车吗？

THINGS YOU'LL SEE

厕所	cèsuǒ	toilet
出口	chūkǒu	exit
候车室	hòuchēshì	waiting room
禁止入内	jìnzhǐ rù nèi	no entry
禁止吸烟	jìnzhǐ xīyān	no smoking
开水	kāishuǐ	boiled water
冷水	léngshuǐ	cold water
全国铁路示意图	quánguó tiělù shìyì tú	All-China railway map
热水	rèshuǐ	hot water
入口	rùkǒu	entrance
售票处	shòupiào chù	ticket office
问讯处	wènxùnchù	information
无人	wúrén	vacant
行李寄存处	xínglǐ jìcún chù	left luggage
洗手间	xíshǒujiān	washroom
站台	zhàntái	platform
站台票	zhàntái piào	platform ticket

THINGS YOU'LL HEAR

Lǚkèmen zhùyì
Attention all passengers

... zhàn bù tíng
does not stop in ...

Chápiào/Jiǎnpiào
Tickets please

Ní mái zǎocān/wǔcān piào ma?
Do you want to buy a breakfast/lunch ticket?

Qíng qǐlái, huàn chuángdān le
Please get up, we want to change the sheets

Háiyǒu ... fēnzhōng, lièchē jiù dàodá ... zhàn le
We arrive in (place) ... in (time) ...

Qíng lǚkèmen jiǎnchá yíxià zìjǐ de xínglǐ
Please check you have all your luggage with you

Zhù dàjiā lǚtú yúkuài
We wish everyone a pleasant journey

AIR TRAVEL

Many international airlines fly to several destinations within China, and, in recent years, the number of international connections has increased considerably. Domestic routes are nearly all flown by CAAC (Civil Aviation Administration of China). The network is extensive and reasonably efficient. There are no return tickets and tickets are bought at the point of departure. It is sometimes possible to persuade a friendly CAAC or CITS office to telex another CAAC office to reserve tickets. Foreigners must pay in FEC, and usually pay considerably more than a Chinese. Although it can sometimes be difficult to buy tickets for a few days ahead, they can be reserved, free of charge, for a flight a few weeks ahead.

USEFUL WORDS AND PHRASES

aircraft fēijī		飞机
air hostess kōngzhōng xiáojiě		空中小姐
airline hángkōng gōngsī		航空公司
airport jīchǎng		机场
airport bus jīchǎng bānchē		机场班车
arrival dàodá		到达
baggage claim xínglǐ tíqǔ chù		行李提取处
boarding card dēngjī pái		登机牌
check-in (verb) bànlǐ dēngjī shǒuxù		办取登机手续
customs hǎiguān		海关
delay wándiǎn		晚点
departure qǐfēi		起飞
departure lounge hòujīshì		候机室

emergency exit	ānquánmén	安全门
flight	hángbān	航班
flight number	hángbān hào	航班号
gate	dēngjīkǒu	登机口
luggage trolley	xínglǐchē	行李车
passport	hùzhào	护照
seat	zuòwèi	座位
seat belt	ānquándài	安全带
steward	nán fúwùyuán	男服务员
stewardess	nǚ fúwùyuán	女服务员

When is there a flight to …?
Qù … de hángbān shì jídiǎn?
去…的航班是几点？

What time does the flight to … leave?
Qù … de hángbān jídián qǐfēi?
去…的航班几点起飞？

Is it a direct flight?
Zhè shì zhídá hángbān ma?
这是直达航班吗？

Do I have to change planes?
Wǒ xūyào huàn jī ma?
我需要换机吗？

When do I have to check in?
Jí diǎnzhōng bànlǐ dēngjī shǒuxù?
几点钟办理登机手续？

I'd like a ticket to ...
Wó xiǎngyào yìzhāng qù ... de jīpiào
我想要一张去…的机票

I'd like a non-smoking seat please
Wó xiǎngyào yíge jìnyānqū de zuòwèi
我想要一个禁烟区的座位

I'd like a window seat please
Wó xiǎngyào yíge kào chuāng de zuòwèi
我想要一个靠窗的座位

How long will the flight be delayed?
Zhège hángbān jiāng wándiǎn duōjiǔ?
这个航班将晚点多久？

Which gate for the flight to ...?
Qù ... de hángbān zài nǎge dēngjīkǒu?
去…的航班在哪个登机口？

When do we arrive in ...?
Wǒmen jí diǎnzhōng dàodá ...?
我们几点钟到达…？

May I smoke now?
Wǒ xiànzài kéyǐ xīyān ma?
我现在可以吸烟吗？

I don't feel very well
Wó gǎnjué bù shūfú
我感觉不舒服

Do you have any more tickets for ...?
Háiyǒu qù ... de jīpiào ma?
还有去…的机票吗？

I want to join the standby queue for today's flight to …
Wó xiáng děng jīntiān qù … de hòubǔ jīpiào
我想等今天去…的候补机票

THINGS YOU'LL SEE

安全门	ānquánmén	emergency exit
办理登机手续	bànlǐ dēngjī shǒuxù	check-in
乘客	chéngkè	passengers
出口	chūkǒu	exit
当地时间	dāngdì shíjiān	local time
到达	dàodá	arrivals
登机口	dēngjīkǒu	gate
国际航线	guójì hángxiàn	international airline
国内航线	guónèi hángxiàn	domestic airline
海关检查	hǎiguān jiǎnchá	customs control
航班	hángbān	flight
护照检查	hùzhào jiǎnchá	passport control
系好安全带	jì hǎo ānquándài	fasten seat belt
紧急降落	jǐnjí jiàngluò	emergency landing
禁烟区	jìnyānqū	non-smokers
免税商店	miǎnshuì shāngdiàn	duty-free shop
起飞	qǐfēi	departures
请不要吸烟	qǐng búyào xīyān	no smoking please
入口	rùkǒu	entrance
问讯处	wènxùnchù	information
行李提取处	xínglǐ tíqǔ chù	baggage claim

→

43

预定航班	yùdìng hángbān	scheduled flight
直达航班	zhídá hángbān	direct flight
中国民航	Zhōngguó Mínháng	CAAC (Civil Aviation Administration of China)

THINGS YOU'LL HEAR

Qù ... de hángbān xiànzài kāishǐ dēngjī
The flight for ... is now boarding

Xiànzài qǐng qù ... hào dēngjīkǒu
Please go now to gate number ...

Qù ... de hángbān wǎndiǎn le
The flight to ... is delayed

BUS, BOAT AND CITY TRANSPORT

In towns and cities there is usually a good bus service, although the buses do tend to stop running rather early (around 11 p.m.). Route maps can be bought on the street from hawkers. Tickets are very cheap and are bought from the conductor on the bus. Cheap monthly tickets for unlimited use within a given area are available from the bus company. Buses tend to be very overcrowded, particularly in the rush hour, as there is no limit to the number of passengers allowed. So be prepared to elbow your way on!

There is also an extensive bus service between towns, although buses don't always stop in the countryside or in small villages to pick up passengers. Travel can be slow and conditions crowded. Many fellow passengers have weak stomachs, so be prepared for their bus-sickness! Single tickets, which are cheap, can be bought at the bus station you are leaving from no more than three days in advance, but return tickets are not available. It is usually reasonably easy to buy bus tickets. Different prices for the same destination indicate the quality of the bus, and it is often advisable to spend a little more on your ticket. On a journey of two or more days, the bus will pull in to a youth hostel-type hotel in the evening. The cost of the overnight stay is not included in the ticket. Buses leave early and promptly the next day, often without waiting for late risers. Bus travel is usually a very pleasant way to travel in China.

There is a modern underground in central Beijing, tickets costing just a few *'jiǎo'*. Within cities, the fastest way to travel is by taxi. These can be hired from hotels or outside tourist sights or hailed on the street. You will often have to pay in FEC (see BANKS AND MONEY). In tourist centres it is usually possible to hire a minibus from hotels for sight-seeing tours.

On navigable rivers there are usually ferries. However, the standard varies, depending on how remote the area is. Large ferries, such as those plying the Changjiang River (Yangtse) or those going to/from Hainan Island, have five classes of accommodation. First class is extremely luxurious, second is a four-berth cabin, third class is a dormitory-type cabin for 8-10 people, fourth class is a large public

45

cabin and fifth class is floor space in the hold. Food on board tends to be bad, so it is advisable to take some of your own. There are also pleasant and cheap evening ferries between Hong Kong and Guangzhou, and this is often the easiest way to travel this route.

USEFUL WORDS AND PHRASES

adult dàrén	大人	
boat chuán	船	
bus gōnggòng qìchē	公共汽车	
bus *(in town)* shìqūchē	市区车	
(suburbs) jiāoqūchē	郊区车	
(long distance) chángtú qìchē	长途汽车	
bus station chēzhàn	车站	
bus stop qìchē zhàn	汽车站	
child értóng	儿童	
coach lǚyóu chē	旅游车	
conductor shòupiàoyuán	售票员	
connection liányùn	联运	
cruise boat yóuchuán	游船	
driver sījī	司机	
fare chēfèi	车费	
ferry dùchuán	渡船	
minibus xiǎo gōnggòng qìchē	小公共汽车	
monthly ticket yuèpiào	月票	
network map jiāotōngtú	交通图	
night bus yèbānchē	夜班车	

number 5 bus wǔ lù gōnggòng qìchē	5 路公共汽车
passenger chéngkè	乘客
port gángkǒu	港口
quay mǎtóu	码头
river jiāng/hé	江／河
sea hǎi	海
seat zuòwèi	座位
station (long-distance bus) chángtú qìchē zhàn	长途汽车站
station (town bus) qìchē zǒng zhàn	汽车总站
station (under-ground) dìtiě zhàn	地铁站
taxi chūzūchē	出租车
ticket chēpiào	车票
underground dìtiě	地铁

Where is the bus station?
Qìchē zǒng zhàn zài nálǐ?
汽车总站在哪里？

Where is there a bus stop?
Nálǐ yǒu qìchē zhàn?
哪里有汽车站？

Where is the number 5 bus stop?
Wǔ lù qìchē zhàn zài nálǐ?
5 路汽车站在哪里？

Which buses go to …?
Qù … zuò jǐ lù chē?
去…坐几路车？

How often do the buses to … run?
Qù … de chē duō cháng shíjiān yítàng?
去…的车多长时间一趟？

Where is the nearest underground station?
Zuì jìn de dìtiě zhàn zài nálǐ?
最近的地铁站在哪里？

Would you tell me when we get to …?
Nǐ néng bù néng dào … zhàn jiào wǒ yíxià?
你能不能到…站叫我一下？

Do I have to get off yet?
Wǒ zài zhèlǐ xiàchē ma?
我在这里下车吗？

How do you get to …?
Qù … zěnme zǒu?
去…怎么走？

Is it very far?
Hén yuǎn ma?
很远吗？

I'd like to go to …
Wó xiǎng qù …
我想去…

Do you go near …?
Nǐ qù … fùjìn ma?
你去…附近吗？

Where can I buy a ticket?
Zài nálǐ mǎi piào?
在哪里买票？

Could you open/close the window?
Nǐ néng bù néng kāi/guān yíxia chuāng?
你能不能开／关一下窗？

Could you help me get a ticket?
Nǐ néng bù néng bāng wó mǎi yì zhāng piào?
你能不能帮我买一张票？

When does the last bus leave?
Mòbān chē shì jídiǎn?
末班车是几点？

When does the first bus leave?
Tóubān chē shì jídiǎn?
头班车是几点？

THINGS YOU'LL SEE

保持车内清洁	bǎochí chē nèi qīngjié	keep the bus tidy
查票员	chápiàoyuán	ticket inspector
出口	chūkǒu	exit
出租汽车站	chūzū qìchē zhàn	taxi rank
后门	hòumén	entry at the rear
加车	jiāchē	extra service (rush hour)
禁止入内	jìnzhǐ rù nèi	no entry
开车时间	kāichē shíjiān	departure →

快车	kuàichē	express bus
老、幼、病、残、孕专座	lǎo, yòu, bìng, cán, yùn zhuānzuò	seats for the elderly, children, the sick, the disabled and pregnant women
路线	lùxiàn	route
码头	mǎtóu	harbour
前门	qiánmén	entry at the front
请勿随地吐痰	qǐng wù suídì tǔtán	no spitting
请勿吸烟	qǐng wù xīyān	no smoking
请勿与司机谈话	qǐng wù yǔ sījī tánhuà	do not speak to the driver
区间车	qūjiānchē	shuttle bus (*only going part of route*)
入口	rùkǒu	entrance
售票处	shòupiàochù	ticket office
司机	sījī	driver
太平门	tàipíngmén	emergency exit
停	tíng	stop
先下后上	xiān xià hòu shàng	allow passengers to alight before boarding
小心扒手	xiǎoxīn páshǒu	beware of pickpockets
终点站	zhōngdiǎnzhàn	terminus
中门	zhōngmén	entry at the middle

BICYCLES

The most practical and pleasant way to travel short distances in China is by bicycle. Bicycles tend to be heavy and gearless but solid and quite fast on the flat. They can be hired from most tourist hotels and also privately, although prices vary considerably. There are cycle repairers – who will also pump up tyres – on many street corners. They usually do a fast, effective and cheap job. Chinese people often cycle very slowly, with little apparent control but, after a while, it is easy to get used to the crowded cycling conditions. Cycle on the right. Traffic coming onto a roundabout has priority. If you are turning right at traffic lights, you just continue and do not have to stop at the lights. In towns and cities, bicycles should be parked in designated bicycle parks. A small fee is charged for parking.

USEFUL WORDS AND PHRASES

basket	kuāng	筐
bell	chēlíng	车铃
bicycle	zìxíngchē	自行车
brakes	shāchē	刹车
chain	liàntiáo	链条
handlebars	chēbǎ	车把
hire	zū	租
inner tube	nèitāi	内胎
lady's bicycle	nǚchē	女车
lock	suǒ	锁
man's bicycle	nánchē	男车
pedal	tàijiǎo	踏脚
pump	dǎqìtǒng	打气筒

BICYCLES

puncture	chuānkǒng	穿孔
saddle	ānzuò	鞍座
spoke	(lún)fú	（轮）辐
tricycle	sānlúnchē	三轮车
tyre	chētāi	车胎
wheel	chēlún	车轮

I'd like to hire a bicycle
Wó xiǎng zū yíliàng zìxíngchē
我想租一辆自行车

How much does it cost for 1 hour/day?
Méi xiǎoshí/měitiān duōshǎo qián?
每小时／每天多少钱？

Do you need a deposit?
Xūyào fù yājin ma?
需要付押金吗？

Could you please mend this puncture?
Qíng bǔ yíxia chētāi
请补一下车胎

Could you please mend the brakes?
Qíng xiū yíxia shāchē
请修一下刹车

Could you pump up the tyres for me?
Qíng nǐ bāng wǒ dǎ yíxia qì, hǎo ma?
请你帮我打一下气，好吗？

Where can I park the bicycle?
Nálǐ kéyǐ tíngfàng zìxíngchē?
哪里可以停放自行车？

How much does it cost to park the bicycle?
Cúnchē yào duōshǎo qián?
存车要多少钱？

Could you raise/lower the saddle?
Nǐ néng bù néng bāng wǒ bǎ chēzuò fàng gāo/fàng dī yíxie?
你能不能帮我把车座放高／放低一些？

THINGS YOU'LL SEE

出租自行车	chūzū zìxíngchē	bicycle hire
存车处	cúnchē chù	cycle park
骑车不准带人	qíchē bùzhǔn dài rén	carrying passengers on a bicycle is not allowed
修理自行车	xiūlǐ zìxíngchē	bicycle repairs
自行车道	zìxíngchē dào	cycle lane
自行车存放处	zìxíngchē cúnfàng chù	cycle park

DOING BUSINESS

Doing business in China is often a painfully slow and frustrating experience for Western companies, used to quick decisions. In China, politics, economics and business are inseparable and industry is very hierarchical. Factories or companies are usually responsible to the relevant provincial level ministry, but exceptionally large or important factories may have to report directly to the relevant ministry in Beijing. Up until late 1988-89, Chinese industry was being decentralized, but due to recent political changes and inflation, this process is presently being reversed. This hierarchical set-up inevitably means that decision-making is lengthy, because any plan agreed at local level must also be agreed, and often altered, at provincial and national level. However, foreign companies trading in China are advised to have direct involvement with the central authorities because their approval gives a measure of protection.

Most ministries, corporations and large factories have their own English interpreters, who usually have a good technical background.

When approaching any level of authority, it is very important to take your business card, clearly stating your position in your company, as status is considered very important. Laying the groundwork for any type of business deal will involve banquets and speeches. If the Chinese hosts invite the Western company to a banquet, it is considered polite for the company's representatives to then host a return banquet a few days later. During a banquet there are always speeches, made by both sides. It is advisable to stress the importance of international friendship and co-operation and mutual assistance. Banquets often involve drinking a lot of *'máotái'* – a Chinese spirit. Be careful of this drink's alcohol content!

USEFUL WORDS AND PHRASES

accept	jiēshòu	接受
accountant	kuàiji	会计

accounts department	cáiwù kē	财务科
advertisement	guǎnggào	广告
advertising	guǎnggào	广告
airfreight *(verb)*	kōngyùn	空运
bid	tóubiāo	投标
board *(of directors)*	dǒngshìhuì	董事会
brochure	xiǎocèzi	小册子
business card	míngpiàn	名片
businessman	shāngrén	商人
chairman *(of company)*	zhǔrèn	主任
cheap	piányi	便宜
company	gōngsī	公司
computer	jìsuànjī	计算机
consumer	xiāofèizhě	消费者
contract	hétóng	合同
cost	chéngběn	成本
customer	gùkè	顾客
director	dǒngshì	董事
discount	jiǎnjià	减价
documents	wénjiàn	文件
down payment	dìngjīn	订金
engineer	gōngchéngshī	工程师
executive	dǒngshì	董事
expensive	guì	贵
exports	chūkǒu shāngpǐn	出口商品
fax	chuánzhēn	传真
import *(verb)*	jìnkǒu	进口
imports	jìnkǒu shāngpǐn	进口商品

instalment	fēnqī fùkuǎn	分期付款
invoice *(noun)*	fāpiào	发票
invoice *(verb)*	kāi fāpiào	开发票
leader	língdǎo	领导
letter	xìn	信
letter of credit	xìnyòng zhèng	信用证
loss	kuīsǔn	亏损
manager	jīnglǐ	经理
manufacture	zhìzào	制造
margin	chā é	差额
market	shìchǎng	市场
marketing	shìchǎng yíngxiāo	市场营销
meeting	huìyì	会议
negotiations	tánpàn	谈判
offer *(quote)*	bàojià	报价
order *(noun)*	dìnghuò dān	订货单
order *(verb)*	dìnghuò	订货
personnel	zhíyuán	职员
price	jiàgé	价格
product	chǎnpǐn	产品
production	shēngchǎn	生产
profit	lìrùn	利润
promotion *(publicity)* xuānchuán		宣传
purchase order	gòuhuò dìngdān	购货订单
sales department	xiāoshòubù	销售部
sales director	yíngyè zhǔrèn	营业主任
sales figures	xiāoshòu'é	销售额

secretary	mìshū	秘书
shipment	zhuāngyùn	装运
tax	shuì	税
telex	diànchuán	电传
tender (noun)	tóubiāo	投标
total	zǒng'é	总额

My name is ...
Wǒ jiào ...
我叫⋯

Here's my card
Zhèshì wǒde míngpiàn
这是我的名片

Pleased to meet you
Hěn gāoxìng rènshi nǐ
很高兴认识你

May I introduce ...?
Wǒ lái jièshào yíxià ...
我来介绍一下⋯

My company is ...
Wǒde gōngsī jiào ...
我的公司叫⋯

Our product is selling very well in the UK market
Wǒmen de chánpǐn zài Yīngguó shìchǎng xiāolù hén hǎo
我们的产品在英国市场销路很好

We are looking for partners in China
Wǒmen zhèng zài Zhōngguó xúnzhǎo màoyì huǒbàn
我们正在中国寻找贸易伙伴

57

At our last meeting ...
Zài wǒmen shàngcì kāihuì shí ...
在我们上次开会时…

10%/25%/50%
Bǎi fēn zhī shí/bǎi fēn zhī èrshíwǔ/bǎi fēn zhī wǔshí
百分之十 ／百分之二十五 ／百分之五十

More than ...
Bǐ ... duō
比…多

Less than ...
Bǐ ... shǎo
比…少

We're on schedule
Wǒmen shì ànshí de
我们是按时的

We're slightly behind schedule
Wǒmen bǐ yùdìng jìhuà wǎnle yìdiǎn
我们比预定计划晚了一点

Please accept our apologies
Qǐng jiēshòu wǒmen de dàoqiàn
请接受我们的道歉

There are good government grants available
Néng dédào xiāngdāng duō de zhèngfǔ zīzhù
能得到相当多的政府资助

It's a deal
Zhèyàng jiù suàn chéngjiāo le
这样就算成交了

I'll have to check that with my chairman
Wǒ bìxū yú wǒmen huìzhǎng héduì yíxià nèige shìqíng
我必须与我们会长核对一下那个事情

I'll get back to you on that
Wǒ huítóu zài gàosù nǐ nèige
我回头再告诉你那个

Our quote will be with you very shortly
Wǒmen de bàojià hěnkuài jiù huì géi nǐmen
我们的报价很快就会给你们

We'll send it by telex
Wǒmen huì dǎ diànchuán de
我们会打电传的

We'll send them airfreight
Wǒmen huì kōngyùn de
我们会空运的

It's a pleasure to do business with you
Wǒmen hěn gāoxìng yú nǐmen yìqǐ zuò shēngyì
我们很高兴与你们一起做生意

**We look forward to a mutually beneficial business
relationship**
Wǒmen qīdài zhe yú nǐmen jiànlì yìzhǒng hùlì de màoyì guānxì
我们期待着与你们建立一种互利的贸易关系

RESTAURANTS

Joint venture hotels have good international cuisine, with excellent service at international prices. Good Chinese hotels also provide meals, paid for separately from the cost of a room – although standards vary. It is, however, much cheaper and often more interesting to eat in one of the very numerous Chinese restaurants. Chinese restaurants are rarely as clean as Western ones, but don't be put off too easily. If lots of Chinese eating there, it probably serves good food. Don't worry about language shortcomings: it's perfectly acceptable to walk into the kitchen and point to whatever you would like to eat. All meals are served with rice and usually with tea. There will be large thermos flasks of boiled water available to top up your cup of tea. Most restaurants sell beer and 'báijiǔ', the fiery Chinese alcohol.

It is not customary to tip, either in restaurants or in hotels. Chinese people eat with chopsticks, but a spoon can be provided on request.

There is little similarity between Chinese food in Britain and Chinese food in China, as the food available in Britain tends to be Cantonese food adapted for the British palate. Food in China varies a great deal between regions and seasons, so it is hard to generalize about flavour. If possible, try local specialities. A Chinese meal rarely includes dessert and usually finishes with soup. Note that Chinese people often eat their rice last. So, if you want rice to accompany the meal, it may be necessary to ask for it specially.

USEFUL WORDS AND PHRASES

beer	píjiǔ	啤酒
bill	zhàngdān	账单
bottle	píngzi	瓶子
bowl	wǎn	碗
chopsticks	kuàizi	筷子

coffee	kāfēi	咖啡
cup	bēizi	杯子
fork	chāzi	叉子
glass	bōlibēi	玻璃杯
hot *(spicy)*	là	辣
knife	dāo	刀
menu	càidān	菜单
milk	niúnǎi	牛奶
plate	pánzi	盘子
rice	mǐfàn	米饭
sandwich	sānmíngzhì	三明治
serviette	cānjin	餐巾
snack	diǎnxīn	点心
soup	tāng	汤
soy sauce	jiàngyóu	酱油
spoon	tiáogēng	调羹
sugar	táng	糖
table	zhuōzi	桌子
tea	chá	茶
teahouse	cháguǎn	茶馆
teaspoon	cháchí	茶匙
waiter	nán fúwùyuán	男服务员
waitress	nǚ fúwùyuán	女服务员
water	shuǐ	水
wine	jiǔ	酒

RESTAURANTS

A table for two please
Qǐng yào yìzhāng liǎngge rén de zhuōzi
请要一张两个人的桌子

Can I see the menu?
Wǒ néng kàn yíxià càidān ma?
我能看一下菜单吗？

I'd like ...
Wó xiǎngyào ...
我想要…

Just a cup of tea, please
Jiù yào yìbēi chá
就要一杯茶

Waiter/waitress!
Fúwùyuán!
服务员！

Can we pay please?
Fùkuǎn
付款

Not too hot (spicy), please
Qǐng búyào tài là
请不要太辣

I didn't order this
Wǒ méiyǒu diǎn zhège
我没有点这个

May we have some more ...?
Wǒmen kéyǐ zài yào yíxiē ... ma?
我们可以再要一些 … 吗？

That was excellent, thank you
Zhè dùn fàn tài hǎo chīle, xièxie nǐ
这顿饭太好吃了，谢谢你

I can't use chopsticks
Wǒ búhuì yòng kuàizi
我不会用筷子

Do you cook with pork fat?
Nǐmen shì bú shì yòng zhūyóu shāo de?
你们是不是用猪油烧的？

I only want vegetables
Wó zhǐ yào shūcài
我只要蔬菜

I am a vegetarian
Wǒ shì chīsù de
我是吃素的

YOU MAY HEAR

Ní xiǎng chīdiǎn shénme?
What would you like?

Nǐ huì yòng kuàizi ma?
Can you use chopsticks?

Nǐ chī làjiāo ma?
Do you eat chilli?

THINGS YOU'LL SEE

菜单	càidān	menu
菜馆	càiguǎn	restaurant
餐厅	cāntīng	restaurant
茶馆	cháguǎn	teahouse (*large*)
茶室	cháshì	teahouse (*small*)
饭店	fàndiàn	restaurant
饭庄	fànzhuāng	restaurant
糕点店	gāodiǎndiàn	cake shop
今日供应	jīnrì gōngyìng	today's menu
酒家	jiǔjiā	restaurant
酒楼	jiǔlóu	restaurant
咖啡店	kāfēidiàn	coffee shop
快餐店	kuàicāndiàn	fast food
冷饮店	lěngyǐndiàn	cold drinks bar
奶制品店	nǎi zhìpǐn diàn	dairy products café (*sells milk, yoghurt, ice cream, cakes, biscuits etc*)
清真饭店	qīngzhēn fàndiàn	Moslem restaurant
收款台	shōukuǎntái	cashier
素菜馆	sùcàiguǎn	vegetarian restaurant
小吃店	xiǎochīdiàn	snack-bar/stall
西餐厅	xīcāntīng	Western-style restaurant
饮食店	yǐnshídiàn	café

RICE AND NOODLES

炒饭	**chǎofàn**	fried rice
炒面	**chǎomiàn**	fried noodles
炒米粉	**chǎomǐfěn**	fried rice noodles
蛋炒饭	**dàn chǎofàn**	fried rice with egg
面条	**miàntiáo**	noodles
米饭	**mǐfàn**	rice
糯米	**nuòmǐ**	glutinous rice
稀饭	**xīfàn**	rice porridge, congee

SOME BASIC FOOD ITEMS

豆沙包	**dòushābāo**	steamed dumpling with sweet bean paste filling
花卷	**huājuǎn**	steamed rolls
馒头	**mántou**	steamed bread
面包	**miànbāo**	bread (white)
肉	**ròu**	meat (usually pork)
咸菜	**xiáncài**	pickles

COOKING METHODS AND BASIC COMBINATIONS

炒…	**chǎo …**	stir-fried …
叉烧…	**chāshāo …**	barbecued …
…丁	**… dīng**	diced …
冬菇…	**dōnggū …**	… with dried mushrooms

咖喱…	**gālí** ...	curried ...
宫保…	**gōngbǎo** ...	stir-fried ... with peanuts and chilli
蚝油…	**háoyóu** ...	... with oyster sauce
红烧…	**hóngshāo** ...	... braised in brown sauce
滑溜…	**huáliū** ...	stir-fried ... with sauce added
烩…	**huì** ...	stewed ...
火锅…	**huǒguō** ...	... in hotpot
火腿…	**huótuǐ** ...	... with ham
家常…	**jiācháng** ...	home-style ...
烤…	**kǎo** ...	roasted ...
…块	**... kuài**	... chunks, pieces
辣子…	**làzi** ...	... with chilli
麻酱…	**májiàng** ...	... quick-fried in sesame paste
麻辣…	**málà** ...	... with chilli and wild pepper
…片	**... piàn**	sliced ...
茄汁…	**qiézhī** ...	... with tomato sauce
清蒸…	**qīngzhēng** ...	steamed ...
三鲜…	**sānxiān** ...	'three-fresh' ... (with 3 ingredients which vary)
…丝	**... sī**	shredded ...
糖醋…	**tángcù** ...	sweet and sour ...
…丸（元）	**... wán** (*or* **yuán**)	... balls
香酥…	**xiāngsū** ...	crispy deep-fried ...

炸…	zhá ...	deep-fried ...
榨菜…	zhàcài ...	... with pickled mustard greens
蒸…	zhēng ...	steamed ...

PORK

叉烧肉	chāshāo ròu	barbecued pork
辣子肉丁	làzi ròudīng	stir-fried diced pork with chilli
米粉蒸肉	mǐfěn zhēngròu	steamed pork with rice
木须炒肉	mùxū chǎoròu	stir-fried sliced pork with eggs, tree-ear (edible fungus) and day lily (type of dried lily)
青椒炒肉片	qīngjiāo chǎo ròupiàn	stir-fried sliced pork with pepper
笋炒肉片	sún chǎo ròupiàn	stir-fried sliced pork with bamboo shoots
糖醋排骨	tángcù páigǔ	sweet and sour spareribs
榨菜炒肉丝	zhàcài chǎo ròusī	stir-fried shredded pork with pickled mustard greens
猪肉	zhūròu	pork

CHICKEN AND DUCK

白斩鸡	báizhǎnjī	sliced cold chicken
北京烤鸭	Běijīng kǎoyā	Peking duck
鸡	jī	chicken
酱爆鸡丁	jiàngbào jīdīng	diced chicken quick-fried with bean sauce

叫化鸡	**jiàohuājī**	'beggar's chicken' (charcoal-baked marinaded chicken)
鸡丁	**jīdīng**	diced chicken
香菇鸭掌	**xiānggū yāzhǎng**	duck's foot with mushroom
鸭	**yā**	duck

BEEF AND LAMB

葱爆牛肉	**cōngbào niúròu**	beef quick-fried with Chinese onions
宫保牛肉	**gōngbǎo niúròu**	stir-fried beef with peanuts and chilli
红烧牛肉	**hóngshāo niúròu**	beef braised in brown sauce
烤羊肉串	**kǎo yángròuchuàn**	kebabs
牛肉	**niúròu**	beef
涮羊肉	**shuàn yángròu**	Mongolian hot-pot
羊肉	**yángròu**	lamb
鱼香牛肉	**yúxiāng niúròu**	stir-fried beef in hot spicy sauce

FISH AND SEAFOOD

芙蓉虾仁	**fúróng xiārén**	stir-fried shrimps with egg white
干烧黄鳝	**gānshāo huángshàn**	paddyfield eel braised with chilli and bean sauce
红烧鲤鱼	**hóngshāo lǐyú**	carp braised in brown sauce

滑溜鱼片	**huáliū yúpiàn**	stir-fried fish slices with thick sauce added
清蒸鲤鱼	**qīngzhēng lǐyú**	steamed carp
糖醋鱼块	**tángcù yúkuài**	sweet and sour fish
虾	**xiā**	shrimps
鱿鱼	**yóuyú**	squid
<u>鱼</u>	**yú**	fish
<u>鱼</u>片	**yúpiàn**	fish slices

SPECIALITIES

包子	**bāozi**	steamed dumplings with minced pork or various fillings
叉烧包	**chāshāobāo**	steamed dumplings with barbecued pork filling
春卷	**chūnjuǎn**	spring rolls
豆腐干	**dòufu gān**	dried bean curd
豆腐皮	**dòufu pí**	dried soya bean cream
腐竹	**fǔzhú**	'bean curd bamboo' (dried soya bean cream, in shape of bamboo)
锅巴豆腐	**guōbā dòufu**	bean curd fried in batter
锅贴	**guōtiē**	fried Chinese ravioli
馄饨	**húntun** (*or* **yúntún** *or* **chāoshǒu**)	small Chinese ravioli in soup

麻婆豆腐	**mápó dòufu**	'pock-marked woman bean curd' (bean curd with minced beef in hot spicy sauce)
三鲜豆腐	**sānxiān dòufu**	'three-fresh' bean curd (with 3 ingredients which vary)
水饺	**shuǐjiǎo**	Chinese ravioli
松花蛋	**sōnghuādàn**	preserved eggs
馅饼	**xiànbǐng**	savoury fritter
小笼包	**xiǎolóngbāo**	steamed dumplings with various fillings
虾仁豆腐	**xiārén dòufu**	bean curd with shrimps
油条	**yóutiáo**	unsweetened doughnut sticks
蒸饺	**zhēngjiǎo**	steamed Chinese ravioli

VEGETABLES

白菜	**báicài**	cabbage
菠菜	**bōcài**	spinach
炒豆芽	**chǎo dòuyá**	stir-fried bean sprouts
炒时菜	**chǎo shícài**	stir-fried seasonal vegetables
冬笋扁豆	**dōngsǔn biǎndòu**	stir-fried French beans with bamboo shoots
花菜	**huācài**	cauliflower
蘑菇	**mógū**	mushroom
茄子	**qiézi**	aubergine
素什锦	**sù shíjǐn**	stir-fried assorted vegetables

土豆	**tǔdòu**	potato
土豆条	**tǔdòutiáo**	chips
鲜蘑豌豆	**xiānmó wāndòu**	stir-fried peas with mushrooms
西红柿	**xīhóngshì**	tomato
西红柿炒鸡蛋	**xīhóngshì chǎo jīdàn**	stir-fried tomato with egg
玉米	**yùmǐ**	sweet corn

SOUPS

菠菜粉丝汤	**bōcài fěnsī tāng**	soup with spinach and vermicelli
三鲜汤	**sānxiān tāng**	'three-fresh' soup (normally prawns, meat and a vegetable)
时菜肉片汤	**shícài ròupiàn tāng**	soup with sliced pork and seasonal vegetables
什锦冬瓜汤	**shíjǐn dōngguā tāng**	winter marrow soup
西红柿鸡蛋汤	**xīhóngshì jīdàn tāng**	soup with eggs and tomato
榨菜肉丝汤	**zhàcài ròusī tāng**	soup with shredded pork and pickled mustard greens
紫菜汤	**zǐcài tāng**	seaweed and dried shrimp soup

FRUIT

菠萝	**bōluó**	pineapple
广柑	**guǎnggān**	Guangdong sweet orange

哈蜜瓜	**hāmìguā**	honeydew melon
桔子（蜜桔）	**júzi (or mìjú)**	tangerine
梨	**lí**	pear
荔枝	**lìzhī**	lychee
苹果	**píngguǒ**	apple
葡萄	**pútao**	grape
香蕉	**xiāngjiāo**	banana
西瓜	**xīguā**	water melon

DESSERTS

八宝饭	**bābǎo fàn**	'eight-treasure' rice pudding (with 8 types of fruit/nuts)
拨丝香蕉	**básī xiāngjiāo**	banana fritters
冰淇淋	**bīngqílín**	ice cream
冰糖银耳	**bīngtáng yín'ěr**	silver tree-ear in syrup (edible fungus)
什锦水果羹	**shíjǐn shuíguǒ gēng**	fruit salad soup
水果色拉	**shuíguǒ sèlā**	fruit salad

DRINKS

白酒	**báijiǔ**	baijiu (white spirit)
茶	**chá**	tea
咖啡	**kāfēi**	coffee
牛奶	**niúnǎi**	milk
啤酒	**píjiǔ**	beer
葡萄酒	**pútaojiǔ**	wine
汽水	**qìshuǐ**	lemonade

SHOPPING

Shopping in China can be frustrating. It can also be an adventure. Large cities and tourist sites have "friendship stores" which were originally designed exclusively for FEC-paying foreigners (see BANKS AND MONEY). These sell a wide variety of national products and imported goods. In recent years Chinese nationals have also been admitted, and some goods can now be bought with RMB.

In larger towns and cities, shops are open from around 8 a.m. to 7 p.m. You should buy things when you first see them, as they may be sold out if you go back a few days later. Each town has a *'bǎihuò/dàlóu'*, a large department store, which usually sells just about everything. In many shops you will be given a price slip by the sales assistant, which you take and pay at another counter, then you take the receipt back to the original assistant to claim your purchase. Unless the shop assistant insists otherwise, pay in RMB.

Shopping for food is best done in the daily open-air market, where fresh food is available cheaply, although there are considerable seasonal variations. Produce is bought in multiples of 'liǎng' (100g), *'jīn'* (500g) and *'gōngjīn'* (1kg). Always pay in RMB in the markets.

In the countryside, the small shops often sell very little other than the basic essentials and rather old sweets and biscuits.

USEFUL WORDS AND PHRASES

butcher's	ròudiàn	肉店
bookshop	shūdiàn	书店
buy	mǎi	买
cake shop	gāodiǎndiàn	糕点店
cheap	piányi	便宜
chemist's	yàodiàn	药店
department store	bǎihuòdàlóu	百货大楼

electrical store diànqì shāngdiàn		电器商店
fashion shízhuāng		时装
florist's huādiàn		花店
foreign language bookshop wàiwén shūdiàn		外文书店
friendship store yǒuyí shāngdiàn		友谊商店
general store bǎihuòdiàn		百货店
hardware shop túchǎndiàn		土产店
ladies' wear nǚzhuāng		女装
market càichǎng		菜场
menswear nánzhuāng		男装
music shop yīnyuè shūdiàn		音乐书店
receipt shōujù		收据
sale jiǎnjià chūshòu		减价出售
sales assistant shòuhuòyuán		售货员
shoe shop xiédiàn		鞋店
shop *(noun)* shāngdiàn		商店
shop *(verb)* qù mǎi dōngxi		去买东西
souvenir shop lǐpǐndiàn		礼品店
spend huāfèi		花费
stationer's wénjùdiàn		文具店
supermarket chāojí shìchǎng		超级市场
tailor's cáiféng		裁缝
till shōukuǎntái		收款台
toyshop wánjùdiàn		玩具店
travel agency (CITS) lǚxíngshè		旅行社

I'd like ...
Wó xiǎngyào ...
我想要…

Do you have ...?
Nǐmen yǒu ... ma?
你们有…吗？

How much is this?
Zhège duōshǎo qián?
这个多少钱？

Where is the ... department?
... guìtái zài nálǐ?
…柜台在哪里？

Do you have any more?
Hái yǒu ma?
还有吗？

I'd like to change this please
Wó xiǎngyào huàn zhège
我想要换这个

Have you anything cheaper?
Hái yǒu gèng piányi de ma?
还有更便宜的吗？

Have you anything larger?
Yǒu dà yìdiǎn de ma?
有大一点的吗？

Have you anything smaller?
Yóu xiǎo yìdiǎn de ma?
有小一点的吗？

75

SHOPPING

Does it come in other colours?
Hái yǒu biéde yánsè ma?
还有别的颜色吗？

Could you wrap it for me?
Nǐ néng bù néng géi wǒ bāo yíxià?
你能不能给我包一下？

Can I have a receipt?
Wǒ néng bù néng yào zhāng shōujù?
我能不能要张收据？

Can I try it (them) on?
Wǒ néng bù néng shì yíxià?
我能不能试一下？

Where do I pay?
Zài nálǐ fùkuǎn?
在哪里付款？

Can I have a refund?
Wó néng bù néng dédào tuìkuǎn?
我能不能得到退款？

I'm just looking
Wó zhǐshì kànkan
我只是看看

I'll come back later
Wǒ guò yíhuìr huílái
我过一会儿回来

I'd like to buy 1kg/500g ...
Wó xiáng mǎi yì gōngjīn/yìjın ...
我想买一公斤／一斤··

How much does it cost per kilo?
Duōshǎo qián yì gōngjīn?
多少钱一公斤？

That's too expensive
Tài guì le
太贵了

That's enough
Gòu le
够了

Can you help me, please?
Nǐ néng bù néng bāngzhù wǒ?
你能不能帮助我？

THINGS YOU'LL SEE

百货大楼	bǎihuòdàlóu	department store
办公用品	bàngōng yòngpǐn	office supplies
部	bù	department
不退不换	bú tuì bú huàn	no exchange or refunds
付食品商店	fùshípǐn shāngdiàn	groceries
服装店	fúzhuāngdiàn	clothes shop
糕点店	gāodiǎndiàn	cake shop
工艺美术商店	gōngyì měishù shāngdiàn	arts and crafts shop
顾客止步	gùkè zhǐ bù	no entry for customers →

价格	jiàgé	price
减价出售	jiǎnjià chūshòu	reduced price
经理办公室	jīnglǐ bàngōng shì	manager's office
咖啡厅	kāfēitīng	café
科技书店	kējì shūdiàn	science and technology bookstore
楼上	lóushàng	upper floor
楼下	lóuxià	lower floor
面包店	miànbāodiàn	bakery
男装	nánzhuāng	menswear
女装	nǚzhuāng	ladies' clothing
请勿用手摸	qǐng wù yòng shǒu mō	please do not touch
收款台	shōukuǎntái	cashier
书店	shūdiàn	bookshop
童装	tóngzhuāng	children's wear
外文书店	wàiwén shūdiàn	foreign language bookstore
玩具	wánjù	toys
文具店	wénjùdiàn	stationer's
闲人免进	xiánrén miǎn jìn	staff only
鞋店	xiédiàn	shoe shop
烟酒店	yānjiǔdiàn	tobacconist's and off-licence
自选商场	zìxuǎn shāngchǎng	self-service store

THINGS YOU'LL HEAR

Méiyǒu
(We) don't have any

Nǐ yào xiē shénme?
What would you like?

Wǒ néng bāng nǐ zuò xiē shénme?
Can I help you?

Nǐ yǒu méi yǒu língqián?
Have you any change?

Duìbuqǐ, méi yǒu le
I'm sorry we're out of stock

Hái yào biéde ma?
Will there be anything else?

Yào bú yào?
Do you want it?

POST OFFICES

Each large town has an international post office, often with English-speaking staff. International parcels must be sent from these post offices. Customs officials must examine the contents of a parcel before it can be sent abroad, so don't seal your parcel before the examination. These post offices also have a poste restante facility, and a parcel collection service, as parcels are not delivered.

Local post offices are painted green, with green post boxes, though airmail should be posted in a blue post box (if available). It is possible to buy international letter stamps at local post offices. Post offices are open seven days a week, in general from 9 a.m. to 6 p.m. The internal postal service tends to be slow. A telegram is faster, quite cheap and can be written in English if posted from a larger, though not necessarily international, post office. Most large hotels also have a small, and often international, post office.

USEFUL WORDS AND PHRASES

airmail	hángkōng yóujiàn	航空邮件
collection	kāixiāng shíjiān	开箱时间
counter	guìtái	柜台
customs form	guānshuìbiǎo	关税表
delivery	sòngxìn	送信
domestic mail	guónèi yóujiàn	国内邮件
express telegram	jiājí diànbào	加急电报
form	biǎogé	表格
international mail	guójì yóujiàn	国际邮件
letter	xìn	信
letter box	xìnxiāng	信箱
mail (noun)	yóujiàn	邮件

package/parcel bāoguǒ		包裹
pillar box yóutǒng		邮筒
printed matter yìnshuāpǐn		印刷品
post (verb) yóujì		邮寄
postage rates yóufèi		邮费
postal order yóuzhèng huìpiào		邮政汇票
postcard míngxìnpiàn		明信片
postcode yóuzhèng biānmǎ		邮政编码
poste-restante dàilǐng yóujiàn		待领邮件
postman yóudìyuán		邮递员
post office yóujú		邮局
registered letter guàhàoxìn		挂号信
stamp yóupiào		邮票
surface mail pǔtōng yóujiàn		普通邮件
telegram diànbào		电报

How much is a letter/postcard to …?
Jì wǎng … de xìn/míngxìnpiàn duōshǎo qián?
寄往…的信／明信片多少钱？

I would like three 8 fen stamps
Wó xiǎngyào sān zhāng bā fēn de yóupiào
我想要三张八分的邮票

I would like to register this letter
Wó xiǎng jì fēng guàhàoxìn
我想寄封挂号信

I would like to send this parcel to …
Wó xiǎng bǎ zhège bāoguǒ jì wǎng …
我想把这个包裹寄往…

POST OFFICES

How long does the post to … take?
Jì wǎng … de yóujiàn yào duōcháng shíjiān?
寄往…的邮件要多长时间？

Where can I post this?
Wǒ kéyǐ zài shénme dìfāng jì zhège?
我可以在什么地方寄这个？

Is there any mail for me?
Yǒu wǒde xìn ma?
有我的信吗？

I'd like to send a telegram
Wó xiǎng pāi ge diànbào
我想拍个电报

This is to go airmail
Zhège yòng hángkōng jì
这个用航空寄

THINGS YOU'LL SEE

请填一下表	qǐng tián yíxià biǎo	please fill in the form
包裹	bāoguǒ	parcels
待领邮件	dàilǐng yóujiàn	poste-restante
电报	diànbào	telegrams
地址	dìzhǐ	address
费用	fèiyòng	charge
挂号信	guàhàoxìn	registered mail
国际邮资	guójì yóuzī	overseas postage
国内邮资	guónèi yóuzī	inland postage →

海关	hǎiguān	customs
航空邮件	hángkōng yóujiàn	airmail
汇款	huìkuǎn	postal orders – dispatch
汇票	huìpiào	postal order
寄信人	jìxìnrén	sender
开箱时间	kāi xiāng shíjiān	collection times
快递	kuàidì	express
明信片	míngxìnpiàn	postcards
取款	qúkuǎn	postal orders – collection
收信人姓名	shōuxìnrén xìngmíng	addressee
信	xìn	letter
信箱	xìnxiāng	letterbox
营业时间	yíngyè shíjiān	opening hours
邮件	yóujiàn	mail
邮局	yóujú	post office
邮票	yóupiào	stamps
邮筒	yóutǒng	pillar box
邮政编码	yóuzhèng biānmǎ	post code
邮资	yóuzī	postage

BANKS AND MONEY

Travellers' cheques and foreign currency can be exchanged at hotel banks or at the Bank of China, which has branches in all tourist cities and employs English-speaking staff. Note that when foreign currency is exchanged, you will receive FEC (foreign exchange currency) and an exchange slip. When leaving the country, any remaining FEC can be changed back to the original currency at the border bank, provided the customer can produce an exchange slip.

To acquire RMB (*rénmínbi*), the currency used by Chinese people, there is a flourishing black market. In tourist areas there are usually touts outside hotels and at tourist sites. Try to be discreet, although the authorities generally seem to turn a blind eye. However, it is technically illegal for foreigners to use RMB. Be aware that RMB cannot be exchanged for hard currency when leaving the country. For rail and air tickets and hotel bills, you are usually asked to pay in FEC. But in markets, shops, cinemas, privately-owned restaurants and buses it is normal to pay in RMB. The FEC price for imported goods or rare products is often lower than the RMB price.

Both RMB and FEC are issued in 1, 2 and 5 '*fēn*' notes and coins, 1, 2 and 5 '*jiǎo*' notes and 1, 2, 5, 10, 50 and 100 '*yuán*' notes. In spoken Chinese, '*jiǎo*' is usually referred to as '*máo*', and '*yuán*' as '*kuài*'.

Credit cards can be used in China, though only in a few places. Large hotels, friendship shops, large CITS offices, important restaurants and banks will generally accept most main cards, but outside major cities, only banks will take them.

USEFUL WORDS AND PHRASES

bank	yínháng	银行
banknote	chāopiào	钞票

change *(verb)* duìhuàn	兑换
cheque zhīpiào	支票
deposit chǔxù	储蓄
exchange rate huìlǜ	汇率
FEC wàihuì duìhuàn quàn	外汇兑换券
foreign exchange wàihuì duìhuàn	外汇兑换
international money order	国际汇票
guójì huìpiào	
Japanese yen rìyuán	日元
money order huìpiào	汇票
pound sterling yīngbàng	英镑
traveller's cheque lǚxíng zhīpiào	旅行支票
US dollar měiyuán	美元

I'd like to change this into ...
Wó xiǎng bǎ zhège huànchéng ...
我想把这个换成…

Can I cash these traveller's cheques?
Wǒ néng bù néng bǎ zhèxie lǚxíng zhīpiào duìhuànchéng
  xiànkuǎn?
我能不能把这些旅行支票兑换成现款？

What is the exchange rate for the pound?
Yīngbàng de huìlǜ shì duōshǎo?
英镑的汇率是多少？

Can you give me RMB for this?
Nǐ néng bù néng fù gěi wǒ rénmínbì?
你能不能付给我人民币？

TELEPHONES

In China, very few private individuals have their own telephone, and the internal phone system tends to be fairly inefficient. International calls can sometimes be made directly, depending on where you are calling to and from. Generally, calls are made through the international operator, who usually speaks English. You can phone either by booking a call through your hotel's operator, or by going to the Post and Telecommunications main office (*yóudiàndàlóu*) and booking a call at the international counter, then waiting for a connection.

Follow the same procedure for internal calls, but be prepared for a lengthy delay and often a bad connection. It is often more convenient to send a telegram (see POST OFFICES).

Recently, public telephone boxes have been installed in the streets, though these are usually only for local calls. From most hotels and work units, local calls are free, but not from public phones.

International calls must be paid in FEC. Internal call rates depend on the distance called and can sometimes be paid in RMB (see BANKS AND MONEY).

USEFUL WORDS AND PHRASES

call *(noun)*	diànhuà	电话
call *(verb)*	dǎ diànhuà	打电话
code	dìqū hàomǎ	地区号码
dial *(verb)*	bōhào	拨号
dialling tone	bōhào xìnhào	拨号信号
directory enquiries	cháhàotái	查号台
engaged	zhànxiàn	占线
extension	(diànhuà) fēnjī	（电话）分机
external phone	wàixiàn diànhuà	外线电话

internal phone	nèixiàn diànhuà	内线电话
international call	guójì chángtú	国际长途
number	diànhuà hàomǎ	电话号码
operator	jiēxiànyuán	接线员
pay-phone	jìfèi diànhuà	计费电话
public phone	gōngyòng diànhuà	公用电话
reverse charge call	duìfāng fùkuǎn	对方付款
telephone	diànhuà	电话
telephone box	diànhuàtíng	电话亭
telephone directory	diànhuà hàomǎ bù	电话号码薄
wrong number	hàomǎ cuòle	号码错了

Where is the nearest phone box?
Zuì jìn de diànhuàtíng zài nálǐ?
最近的电话亭在哪里？

Can you tell me the number for …?
Néng bù néng gàosù wǒ … de diànhuà hàomǎ?
能不能告诉我…的电话号码？

Can I call abroad from here?
Zhèlǐ néng bù néng guà guójì chángtú?
这里能不能挂国际长途？

I would like to reverse the charges
Wó xiǎng jiào duìfāng fùkuǎn
我想叫对方付款

How long will I have to wait for a connection?
Yào duōcháng shíjiān néng jiētōng?
要多长时间能接通？

Hello, this is … speaking
Wèi, wǒ shì …
喂，我是…

Is that …?
Nǐ shì … ma?
你是…吗？

Please speak slowly
Qǐng shuō màn yíxie
请说慢一些

Speaking
Wǒ jiù shì
我就是

I would like to speak to …
Wó xiáng zhǎo … jiē diànhuà
我想找…接电话

Please tell him … called
Qíng zhuǎngào tā, … géi tā dǎ diànhuà le
请转告他，…给他打电话了

Could you ask her to call me back please
Qǐng ràng tā géi wǒ huíge diànhuà
请让她给我回个电话

My number is …
Wǒde diànhuà hàomǎ shì …
我的电话号码是

Do you know where he is?
Nǐ zhīdào tā zài nálǐ ma?
你知道他在哪里吗？

When will he be back?
Tā shénme shíhòu huílái?
他什么时候回来？

Could you leave him a message?
Néng bù néng gěi tā liú ge tiáozi?
能不能给他留个条子？

I'll ring back later
Wǒ guò yíhuir zài dǎ
我过一会儿再打

Sorry, wrong number
Duìbuqǐ, hàomǎ cuòle
对不起，号码错了

I can't hear you
Wǒ tīng bù qīng
我听不清

THINGS YOU'LL SEE

长途电话	chángtú diànhuà	long-distance calls
电话	diànhuà	telephone
电话亭	diànhuàtíng	telephone box
地区号	dìqūhào	code
公用电话	gōngyòng diànhuà	public phone

国际电话	guójì diànhuà	international calls
坏了	huàile	out of order
郊区电话	jiāoqū diànhuà	local/district calls
接线员	jiēxiànyuán	operator
市内电话	shìnèi diànhuà	local calls (*inside city*)
收费	shōufèi	charges
直拨电话	zhíbō diànhuà	direct dialling

REPLIES YOU MAY BE GIVEN

Ní zhǎo shuí?
Who would you like to speak to?

Shì ni fùkuǎn ma?
Are you paying for the call yourself?

Shì duìfāng fùkuǎn ma?
Is this a reverse call?

Ní bǎ hàomǎ gǎo cuò le
You've got the wrong number

Ní dǎ shénme hàomǎ?
What number are you calling?

Ni shì shuí ya?
Who's speaking?

Wèi
Hello

→

90

Nǐde diànhuà hàomǎ shì duōshǎo?
What is your number?

Duìbuqǐ, tā bú zài
Sorry, he's/she's not in

Tā ... diǎnzhōng huílái
He'll/she'll be back at ... o'clock

Qǐng nǐ míngtiān zài dǎ lái ba
Please call again tomorrow

Wǒ huì gàosù tā nǐ láiguò diànhuà le
I'll tell him/her you called

HEALTH

The standard of health care in China varies dramatically depending on who you are and where you are, but be prepared for rather basic conditions, if comparing to Western standards.

Most hotels have a doctor to whom guests are referred and it is advisable to see this doctor first. If you continue to feel ill, ask for advice on which hospital to go to. If you think you may be seriously ill, try to insist on being admitted to the cadre (*gànbù*) section of a good hospital, as conditions there are generally much better.

Before seeing a doctor, you must report to the hospital registration desk, where you will pay a small fee (RMB) and receive a booklet to give to the doctor. In most Chinese hospitals, there is no appointment system – it's a matter of joining the relevant queue. Consultations are rarely in private, but it is possible to close the door yourself, if it would make things easier for you.

Once admitted to hospital, it is common practice to link the patient to an IV drip, usually glucose. Drips and injections are used a lot in Chinese hospitals, which can be quite upsetting for a foreigner. Often there will be no meals, so you may have to arrange for friends to bring food to you. Chinese doctors often avoid telling the patient exactly what is wrong, particularly if the illness is serious, but he or she will usually discuss the case a little more openly with a friend of the patient. If necessary, the hospital will be able to find an interpreter for you.

Medicine can be bought in a hospital with a prescription or from a chemist with or without a prescription. Hospital treatment involving a stay in hospital varies in cost, and the precise cost is often hard to establish until the bill is presented. Both treatment and medicine are, however, usually cheaper than in Western countries. Foreigners are expected to pay in FEC.

Doctors may ask if you would prefer Western or Chinese medicine and treatment. On the whole, Chinese medicine uses natural products. There are Chinese medicine hospitals in most towns and these usually welcome foreign patients. Chinese medicine prescriptions can only be collected from a Chinese medicine chemist.

USEFUL WORDS AND PHRASES

abscess	nóngzhǒng	脓肿
accident	shìgù	事故
acupuncture	zhēnjiǔ	针灸
ambulance	jiùhùchē	救护车
appendicitis	lánwěiyán	阑尾炎
aspirin	āsīpǐlín	阿斯匹林
asthma	xiāochuǎn	哮喘
backache	bèiténg	背疼
bandage	bēngdài	绷带
bite	yǎoshāng	咬伤
blood	xuè	血
blood pressure	xuèyā	血压
burn	shāoshāng	烧伤
cancer	ái	癌
chemist	yàofáng	药房
chest	xiōngqiāng	胸腔
chickenpox	shuǐdòu	水痘
Chinese medicine	zhōngyào	中药
cold *(noun)*	gǎnmào	感冒
concussion	nǎozhèndàng	脑震荡
constipation	biànbì	便秘
cough	késòu	咳嗽
cut	dāoshāng	刀伤
dentist	yákē yīshēng	牙科医生
doctor	yīshēng	医生
earache	ěrduoténg	耳朵疼

fever	fāshāo	发烧
filling	bǔyá	补牙
first aid	jíjiù	急救
flu	liúxíngxìng gǎnmào	流行性感冒
fracture	gǔzhé	骨折
haemorrhage	nèi chūxuè	内出血
hayfever	huāfěnrè	花粉热
headache	tóuténg	头疼
heart	xīnzàng	心脏
heart attack	xīnzàngbìng	心脏病
hepatitis	gānyán	肝炎
hospital	yīyuàn	医院
ill	shēngbìng	生病
indigestion	xiāohuà bù liáng	消化不良
injection	dǎzhēn	打针
itch	yǎng	痒
kidney	shènzàng	肾脏
measles	mázhěn	麻疹
migraine	piāntóutòng	偏头痛
mumps	liúxíngxìng sāixiànyán	流行性腮腺炎
nausea	ěxīn	恶心
nurse	hùshì	护士
operation	shǒushù	手术
optician	yǎnkē yīshēng	眼科医生
pain	téng	疼
penicillin	pánníxīlín	盘尼西林
plaster (*sticking*)	gāo yào	膏药
plaster of Paris	shóushígāo	熟石膏

pneumonia fèiyán 肺炎

pregnant huáiyùn 怀孕

prescription yàofāng 药方

rheumatism fēngshībìng 风湿病

septic huànóng 化脓

sore téng 疼

sore throat sǎngziténg 嗓子疼

sprain niǔshāng 扭伤

sting cìtòng 刺痛

stomach wèi 胃

temperature tǐwēn 体温

tonsils biǎntáoxiàn 扁桃腺

toothache yáténg 牙疼

travel sickness yùnchē 晕车

ulcer kuìyáng 溃疡

vaccination yùfáng jiēzhǒng 预防接种

Western medicine xīyào 西药

X-ray 'X' guāng "爱克斯"光

I have a pain in ...
Wǒ ... téng
我…疼

I feel sick
Wó gǎndào ěxīn
我感到恶心

I feel dizzy
Wǒ tóuyūn
我头晕

95

I would like to go the cadres' wing
Wó xiǎng qù gāogàn bìngfáng
我想去高干病房

I don't want an IV drip
Wǒ bù xiǎngyào shūyè
我不想要输液

It hurts here
Zhèli téng
这里疼

How do I take the medicine?
Zhège yào zěnme fúfǎ?
这个药怎么服法？

It's a sharp pain
Téng de lìhài
疼得厉害

It's a dull pain
Yǐnyin de téng
隐隐的疼

It hurts all the time
Yìzhí téng
一直疼

It only hurts now and then
Yǒude shíhòu téng
有的时候疼

It hurts when you touch it
Pèng shí téng
碰时疼

96

It hurts more at night
Wǎnshàng téng de gèng lìhài
晚上疼得更厉害

It stings
Xiàng zhēnzhā yíyàng téng
象针扎一样疼

It aches
Suānténg
酸疼

I have a temperature
Wǒ fāshāole
我发烧了

I need a prescription for ...
Wǒ xūyào kāi yíge zhì ... de yàofāng
我需要开一个治…的药方

Please explain what is wrong with me
Qǐng gàosù wǒ shì shénme máobìng
请告诉我是什么毛病

I normally take ...
Wǒ tōngcháng yòng ...
我通常用…

Where can I have a shower?
Línyù zài nálǐ?
淋浴在哪里？

I'm allergic to ...
Wǒ duì ... guòmǐn
我对…过敏

Have you got anything for …?
Ní yǒu zhì … de yào ma?
你有治…的药吗？

I have lost a filling
Wǒde yá bǔguò yòu diào le
我的牙 补过又掉了

Where can I buy this medicine?
Nálǐ néng mǎidào zhège yào?
哪里能买到这个药？

Can I pay for the medicine here?
Wǒ zài zhèli fù yàoqián ma?
我在这里付药钱吗？

I want to register to see the doctor
Wó xiǎng guà ge hào
我想挂个号

Can I see an English-speaking doctor?
Wǒ néng bù néng zhǎoge huì shuō Yīngyǔ de yīshēng?
我能不能找个会说英语的医生？

THINGS YOU'LL HEAR

Nǐ nálǐ bù shūfú?
What seems to be the problem?

Nǐ guàhào le ma?
Have you registered at the front desk?

THINGS YOU'LL SEE

儿科	érkē	paediatrics
妇科	fùkē	gynaecology
挂号处	guàhàochù	registration desk
骨科	gǔkē	orthopaedics
救护车	jiùhùchē	ambulance
内科	nèikē	medical
取药处	qǔyàochù	prescription collection office
外科	wàikē	surgery
五官科	wǔguānkē	ear, nose and throat specialist
"爱克斯"光	'X' guāng	X-ray
药方	yàofāng	prescription
医务所	yīwùsuǒ	clinic
医院	yīyuàn	hospital
值班药剂师	zhíbān yàojìshī	duty chemist
中医科	zhōngyīkē	Chinese medicine department
专家门诊	zhuānjiā ménzhěn	specialist clinic (*Chinese medicine*)

MINI DICTIONARY

a yígè   一个
accident shìgù   事故
adaptor *(plug)* duōyòng chātóu   多用插头
address dìzhǐ   地址
after yǐhòu   以后
again zài   再
air-conditioning kōngtiáo   空调
airport fēijīchǎng   飞机场
alarm clock nàozhōng   闹钟
alcohol jiǔjīng   酒精
all suóyǒu   所有
  all the streets suóyǒu de jiēdào   所有的街道
  that's all, thanks hǎole, xièxie   好了，谢谢
almost chàbuduō   差不多
alone dāndú   单独
already yǐjīng   已经
also yě   也
always zǒngshì   总是
America Měiguó   美国
American *(adj)* Měiguó   美国
and hé   和
another *(different)* lìng yígè   另一个
  (further) yòu yígè   又一个
antibiotics kàngjūnsù   抗菌素
antiseptic fángfǔjì   防腐剂
apartment dānyuán   单元

apple píngguǒ	苹果	
arm gēbo	胳膊	
arrive dàodá	到达	
art yìshù	艺术	
ashtray yānhuīgāng	烟灰缸	
asleep: he's asleep tā shuìzháo le	他睡着了	
at zài	在	
at the café zài kāfēi guǎn	在咖啡馆	
attractive mírénde	迷人的	
aunt *(maternal)* yímā	姨妈	
(paternal) gūmā	姑妈	
Australia Àodàlìyà	澳大利亚	
Australian *(adj)* Àodàlìyà de	澳大利亚的	
awful zāotòule	糟透了	
baby yīng'ér	婴儿	
back *(body)* bèi	背	
back street hòujiē	后街	
bad huài	坏	
ball qiú	球	
bamboo zhúzi	竹子	
bamboo shoots zhúsǔn	竹笋	
banana xiāngjiāo	香蕉	
band *(music)* yuèduì	乐队	
bandage bēngdài	绷带	
bank yínháng	银行	
bar jiǔbā	酒吧	
barber lǐfàshī	理发师	
bath xízǎo	洗澡	

bathroom xǐzǎojiān	洗澡间
battery diànchí	电池
beach hǎitān	海滩
beans dòu	豆
beard húzi	胡子
beautiful *(in appearance)* měilì	美丽
because yīnwèi	因为
bed chuáng	床
bedroom wòshì	卧室
beef niúròu	牛肉
beer píjiǔ	啤酒
before zài ... yǐqián	在…以前
begin kāishǐ	开始
behind zài ... hòumiàn	在…后面
bell zhōng	钟
(for door, school) líng	铃
below zài ... xiàmiàn	在…下面
belt *(clothing)* yāodài	腰带
best: the best zuìhǎo	最好
better gèng hǎo	更好
between zài ... zhījiān	在…之间
bicycle zìxíngchē	自行车
big dà	大
bikini bǐjīní	比基尼
bill zhàngdān	账单
birthday shēngrì	生日
happy birthday! shēngrì kuàilè!	生日快乐！
biscuit bǐnggān	饼干

bitter *(taste)* kǔ 苦

black hēi 黑

blanket tǎnzi 毯子

blind xiā 瞎

blinds bǎiyè chuāng 百叶窗

blocked *(road, drain)* dǔzhùle 堵住了

blond *(adj)* jīnhuángsè 金黄色

blouse nǚchènshān 女衬衫

blue lánsè 蓝色

boat chuán 船

body shēntǐ 身体

boiled rice mǐfàn 米饭

book *(noun)* shū 书

bookshop shūdiàn 书店

boot *(on foot)* xuēzi 靴子

   (car) xínglǐxiāng 行李箱

border *(of country)* biānjiè 边界

boring méi jìn 沒劲

boss láobǎn 老板

both liǎngge dōu 两个都

bottle píngzi 瓶子

bottle-opener píng gài kāi dāo 瓶盖开刀

bowl wǎn 碗

box hézi 盒子

boxer quánjīshǒu 拳击手

boy nánhái 男孩

boyfriend nán péngyǒu 男朋友

bra xiōngzhào 胸罩

bracelet	shǒuzhuó	手镯
brandy	báilándì	白兰地
bread	miànbāo	面包
breakfast	zǎofàn	早饭
bridge *(over river etc)*	qiáo	桥
briefcase	gōngwénbāo	公文包
Britain	Yīngguó	英国
British *(adj)*	Yīngguó	英国
broken *(out of order)*	huàile	坏了
(leg)	duànle	断了
brooch	xiōngzhēn	胸针
brother	xiōngdì	兄弟
brown	zōngsè	棕色
bruise	shānghén	伤痕
brush	shuāzi	刷子
Buddha	Fó	佛
building	fángzi	房子
bulb *(light)*	dēng pào	灯泡
bungalow	píngfáng	平房
burglar	qièzéi	窃贼
Burma	Miǎndiàn	缅甸
burn *(noun)*	shāoshāng	烧伤
bus	gōnggòng qìchē	公共汽车
business	shēngyì	生意
business man	shāngrén	商人
bus station	gōnggòng qìchē zǒng zhàn	公共汽车总站
bus stop	chēzhàn	车站

busy (*street*) rènào 热闹
   (*restaurant*) hěn máng 很忙
but dànshì 但是
butter huángyóu 黄油
button niǔkòu 纽扣
buy mǎi 买
by yóu 由
  by train/car zuò huǒchē/xiǎo qìchē 坐火车／小汽车

café kāfēiguǎn 咖啡馆
cake dàngāo 蛋糕
calculator jìsuànqì 计算器
call: what is this called? zhè jiào shénme? 这叫什么？

camera zhàoxiàngjī 照相机
can (*tin*) guàntou 罐头
can: can I ...? wǒ kéyǐ ... ma? 我可以…吗？
  can you ...? nǐ néng bù néng ...? 你能不能…？
  he can't ... tā bù néng ... 他不能…
Canada Jiānádà 加拿大
Cantonese (*adjective*) Guǎngdōng 广东
  (*language*) Guǎngdōnghuà 广东话
cap màozi 帽子
car xiǎo qìchē 小汽车
card (*business*) míngpiàn 名片
careful: be careful! xiǎoxīn! 小心！
car park tíngchēchǎng 停车场
carpet dìtǎn 地毯

cash *(money)* xiànjīn		现金
cassette cídài		磁带
centre *(of town)* zhōngxīn		中心
chair yǐzi		椅子
change *(noun: money)* língqián		零钱
(verb: money) duì huàn		兑换
(verb: clothes, trains) huàn		换
cheap piányi		便宜
cheers! gānbēi		干杯！
cheese nǎilào		奶酪
chef chúshī		厨师
chemist's yàofáng		药房
cheque zhīpiào		支票
cheque book zhīpiàoběn		支票本
cheque card zhīpiàokǎ		支票卡
chess xiàngqí		象棋
chest *(body)* xiōngkǒu		胸口
chewing gum kǒuxiāngtáng		口香糖
chicken jī		鸡
(meat) jīròu		鸡肉
child, children háizi		孩子
chilli pepper làjiāofěn		辣椒粉
China Zhōngguó		中国
China tea Zhōngguó chá		中国茶
Chinese *(adjective)* Zhōngguo		中国
(person) Zhōngguórén		中国人
(language) Hànyǔ		汉语
the Chinese Zhōngguó rénmín		中国人民

Chinese-style Zhōngshì	中式
chips zhá tǔdòutiáo	炸土豆条
chocolate qiǎokelì	巧克力
chopsticks kuàizi	筷子
church jiàotáng	教堂
cigar xuějiā	雪茄
cigarette xiāng yān	香烟
cinema diànyǐngyuàn	电影院
city chéngshì	城市
clean *(adjective)* gānjìng	干净
clever cōngming	聪明
clock zhōng	钟
close: to be close *(near)* jìn	近
closed guānle	关了
clothes yīfu	衣服
clothes peg yīfu jiāzi	衣服夹子
coast hǎibīn	海滨
coat *(overcoat)* dàyī	大衣
(jacket) wàiyī	外衣
coathanger yījià	衣架
cockroach zhānglāng	蟑螂
coconut yēzi	椰子
coconut milk yēzi zhī	椰子汁
coffee kāfēi	咖啡
cold lěng	冷
I have a cold wó gǎnmàole	我感冒了
collect call duìfāng fùkuǎn	对方付款
colour yánsè	颜色

comb shūzi   梳子
come lái   来
   I come from ... wǒ lái zì ...   我来自…
   come in! qǐng jìn   请进
Communist Party gòngchándǎng   共产党
Communist Party member   共产党员
  gòngchándǎngyuán
company *(firm)* gōngsī   公司
complicated fùzá   复杂
computer jìsuànjī   计算机
concert yīnyuèhuì   音乐会
condom bìyùntào   避孕套
consulate lǐngshìguǎn   领事馆
contact lenses yǐnxíng yǎnjìng   隐形眼镜
cool *(day, weather)* liángkuai   凉快
corner: on the corner guǎijiǎo   拐角处
  chù
  in the corner zài jiǎoluò lǐ   在角落里
cost jià qián   价钱
  what does it cost? zhè yào   这要多少钱？
  duōshǎo qián?
cot diào chuáng   吊床
cotton miánhuā   棉花
cotton wool yàomián   药棉
cough *(verb)* késou   咳嗽
country *(nation)* guójiā   国家
crab pángxiè   螃蟹
cramp jìngluán   痉挛

cream *(to eat)* nǎiyóu	奶油
credit card xìnyòng kǎ	信用卡
crisps zhá tǔdòupiàn	炸土豆片
crocodile èyú	鳄鱼
crowd rénqún	人群
Cultural Revolution Wénhuà Dàgémìng	文化大革命
cup bēizi	杯子
a cup of coffee yī bēi kāfēi	一杯咖啡
curry gālí	咖喱
curtains chuānglián	窗帘
Customs hǎiguān	海关
cut qiè	切
cyclist qí zìxíngchē de rén	骑自行车的人
dangerous wēixiǎn	危险
dark hēi àn	黑暗
daughter nǚ'ér	女儿
day bái tiān	白天
dead sǐle	死了
deaf ěr lóng	耳聋
dear *(expensive)* guì	贵
deep shēn	深
delicious hǎochī	好吃
dentist yákē yīshēng	牙科医生
deodorant chúchòujì	除臭剂
departure chūfā	出发
develop *(film)* chōngxǐ	冲洗
diary rìjì	日记

dictionary zìdiǎn	字典
die sǐ	死
different bùtóng	不同
difficult kùnnan	困难
dinner wǎnfàn	晚饭
dirty zāng	脏
disabled cánfèi	残废
disco dísīkē	迪斯科
divorced líhūnle	离婚了
do zuò	做
doctor yīshēng	医生
dog gǒu	狗
dollar měiyuán	美元
don't! búyào!	不要！
door mén	门
down: down there xiàmiàn nàlǐ	下面那里
dress (*woman's*) liányīqún	连衣裙
drink (*verb*) hē	喝
drinking water yǐnyòngshuǐ	饮用水
driving licence jiàshǐ zhízhào	驾驶执照
drunk zuì	醉
dry gān	干
dry-cleaner's gānxǐdiàn	干洗店
dynasty cháo dài	朝代
the Ming/Ch'ing Dynasty Míngcháo/Qīngcháo	明朝／清朝

each měi yíge	每一个
ear ěrduo	耳朵
early zǎo	早
earring ěrhuán	耳环
east dōng	东
easy róngyì	容易
eat chī	吃
egg jīdàn	鸡蛋
egg noodles jīdàn miàn	鸡蛋面
either ... or ... bú shì ... jiùshi ...	…不是…就是…
elastic yǒu tánxìng de	有弹性的
elastic band sōngjǐndài	松紧带
electricity diàn	电
else: something else biéde dōngxi	别的东西
somewhere else biéde dìfāng	别的地方
embarrassing gāngà	尴尬
embassy dàshíguǎn	大使馆
emergency jǐnjí qíngkuàng	紧急情况
emperor huángdì	黄帝
empty kōng	空
end *(noun)* mòduān	末端
engaged *(toilet)* yǒurén	有人
(person) dìnghūnle	订婚了
England Yīnggélán	英格兰
English *(adj)* Yīnggélán	英国
(language) Yīngyǔ	英语
enough gòule	夠了
entrance rùkǒu	入口

envelope	xìnfēng	信封
evening	wǎnshàng	晚上
every	měiyíge	每一个
everyone	měiyíge rén	每一个人
everything	měijiàn shìqíng	每件事情
everywhere	měige dìfāng	每个地方
excellent	hǎojíle	好极了
excuse me *(to get attention)*	láo jià	劳驾
(pardon?)	qǐng zài shuō yíbiàn, hǎo ma?	请再说一遍，好吗？
exit	chūkǒu	出口
expensive	guì	贵
eye	yǎnjīng	眼睛
face	liǎn	脸
factory	gōngchǎng	工厂
family	jiātíng	家庭
fan *(mechanical)*	fēngshàn	风扇
(hand held)	shànzi	扇子
far (away)	yuǎn	远
farmer	nóngmín	农民
fashion	liúxíng shìyàng	流行式样
fast	kuài	快
fat *(person)*	pàng	胖
father	bàba	爸爸
feel	gǎnjué	感觉
I feel hot	wǒ juéde rè	我觉得热
ferry	dùchuán	渡船
fever	fāshāo	发烧

few: a few yìxiē — 一些

fiancé(e) wèi hūn fū/qī — 未婚夫／妻

field tiándì — 田地

   (rice, paddy) dàotián — 稻田

film *(camera)* jiāojuǎn — 胶卷

   (cinema) diànyǐng — 电影

find zhǎo — 找

finger shǒu zhítou — 手指头

fire huǒ — 火

   there's a fire! zháohuǒ la! — 着火啦！

fire extinguisher mièhuǒqì — 灭火器

first dìyī — 第一

fish yú — 鱼

fisherman yúmín — 渔民

fishing diàoyú — 钓鱼

fishing boat yúchuán — 渔船

fizzy yǒuqìde — 有汽的

flash *(for camera)* shǎnguāngdēng — 闪光灯

flat *(noun)* dānyuán — 单元

flat *(adjective)* píngtǎn — 平坦

flavour wèidao — 味道

flea tiàozǎo — 跳蚤

flight hángbān — 航班

floor *(of room)* dìbǎn — 地板

   (storey) lóu — 楼

flower huā — 花

fly *(insect)* cāngying — 苍蝇

fly *(verb)* fēi — 飞

folk music mínjiān yīnyuè	民间音乐
food shíwù	食物
food poisoning shíwù zhòngdú	食物中毒
foot jiǎo	脚
football zúqiú	足球
for: for her wèi tā	为她
that's for me zhè shì géi wǒde	这是给我的
a bus for ... qù ... de gōnggòng qìchē	去…的公共汽车
forbidden jìnzhǐ	禁止
Forbidden City Zǐjìnchéng	紫禁城
foreigner wàiguoren	外国人
forest sēnlín	森林
fortnight liǎngge xīngqi	两个星期
free zìyóu	自由
(of charge) miǎnfèi	免费
freezer bīngguì	冰柜
fridge bīngxiāng	冰箱
fried noodles chǎomiàn	炒面
fried rice chǎofàn	炒饭
friend péngyǒu	朋友
friendly yóuhǎo	友好
friendship store yǒuyí shāngdiàn	友谊商店
from: from Beijing to Shanghai cóng Běijīng dào Shànghǎi	从北京到上海
front qiánmiàn	前面
fruit shuíguǒ	水果

fruit juice guǒzhī	果汁
fry *(deep fry)* zhá	炸
(stir fry) chǎo	炒
full mǎn	满
I'm full wó bǎole	我饱了
funny *(strange)* qíguài	奇怪
(amusing) yǒu yìsi	有意思
garden huāyuán	花园
garlic dàsuàn	大蒜
gay *(homosexual)* gǎo tóngxìngliàn de	搞同性恋的
gents *(toilet)* nán cèsuǒ	男厕所
get *(obtain)* dé dào	得到
(fetch) qǔ	取
(train, bus etc) zuòchē	坐车
have you got …? ní yǒu … ma?	你有…吗？
get in *(to car)* shàngchē	上车
(arrive) dàodá	到达
get up *(in morning)* qǐchuáng	起床
ginger shēngjiāng	生姜
girl nǚhái	女孩
girlfriend nǚpéngyǒu	女朋友
give gěi	给
glad gāoxìng	高兴
glass *(for drinking)* bōlibēi	玻璃杯
(material) bōli	玻璃
glasses *(spectacles)* yǎnjìng	眼镜

glue jiāoshuǐ	胶水
go qù	去
Gobi Desert Gēbìtān	戈壁滩
gold huángjīn	黄金
good hǎo	好
goodbye zàijiàn	再见
government zhèngfǔ	政府
granddaughter *(son's daughter)* sūnnǚ	孙女
(daughter's daughter) wàisūnnǚ	外孙女
grandfather *(maternal)* wàigōng	外公
(paternal) yéye	爷爷
grandmother *(maternal)* wàipó	外婆
(paternal) nǎinai	奶奶
grandson *(son's son)* sūnzi	孙子
(daughter's son) wài sūnzi	外孙子
grapes pútao	葡萄
grass cǎo	草
great: that's great! hǎojíle	好极了！
Great Britain Dàbùlièdiān	大不列颠
green lǜsè	绿色
green Chinese onion dàcōng	大葱
grey huīsè	灰色
ground floor yī lóu	一楼
guide dǎoyóu	导游
guidebook dǎoyóu shǒucè	导游手册
gun *(pistol)* shǒuqiāng	手枪
(rifle) qiāng	枪

hair tóufa	头发
haircut lǐfà	理发
hairdresser lǐfàshī	理发师
hairdryer diànchuīfēng	电吹风
half yíbàn	一半
ham huótuǐ	火腿
hamburger hànbǎobāo	汉堡包
hammer chuízi	锤子
hand shǒu	手
handbag shǒutíbāo	手提包
handkerchief shǒujuàn	手绢
handle *(noun)* báshǒu	把手
handsome yīngjùn	英俊
happy kuàilè	快乐
harbour gángkǒu	港口
hard *(material)* yìng	硬
(difficult) nán	难
hat màozi	帽子
have yǒu	有
do you have ...? ní yǒu ... ma?	你有…吗？
I don't have ... wǒ méiyǒu ...	我没有…
hay fever huāfěnrè	花粉热
he tā	他
head tóu	头
headache tóuténg	头疼
headlights chētóudēng	车头灯
hear tīngjiàn	听见
hearing aid zhùtīngqì	助听器

heart xīnzàng	心脏
heat rè	热
heavy zhòng	重
heel *(shoe)* xiégēn	鞋跟
(foot) jiǎogēn	脚跟
hello ní hǎo	你好
help *(verb)* bāngzhù	帮助
help! jiùmìng!	救命！
her *(possessive)* tāde	她的
(object) tā	她
herbs *(cooking)* zuǒliào	佐料
(medicine) cǎoyào	草药
here zhèlǐ	这里
hers tāde	她的
hi! ní hǎo!	你好！
high gāo	高
hill xiǎoshān	小山
him tā	他
hire: for hire chūzū	出租
his tāde	他的
holiday jiàqī	假期
(public) jiérì	节日
Hong Kong Xiānggǎng	香港
horrible kěpà	可怕
hot rè	热
(to taste) là	辣
hotel *(superior, for foreigners)*	饭店
fàndiàn	

(small) lǚguǎn 旅馆

house fángzi 房子

how? zěnme? 怎么？

hungry: I'm hungry wǒ èle 我饿了

hurry: I'm in a hurry wǒ méi shíjiān 我沒时间

husband zhàngfu 丈夫

I wǒ 我

ice bīng 冰

ice cream bīngqílín 冰淇淋

if rúguǒ 如果

ill shēng bìngle 生病了

immediately mǎshàng 马上

impossible bù kěnéng 不可能

in zài 在

in English yòng Yīngyǔ 用英语

India Yìndù 印度

infection gǎnrǎn 感染

information xìnxī 信息

insect repellent qūchóngjì 驱虫剂

insurance báoxiǎn 保险

interesting yǒu yìsi 有意思

interpret zuò fānyì 做翻译

Ireland Ài'ěrlán 爱尔兰

iron *(for clothes)* yùndǒu 熨斗

island dǎo 岛

it tā 它

  it's expensive guì 贵

119

jack *(for car)* qiānjīndǐng	千斤顶
jacket wàitào	外套
jade yù	玉
Japan Rìběn	日本
jasmine tea mòlì huā chá	茉莉花茶
jeans niúzǎikù	牛仔裤
jewellery shǒushì	首饰
job gōngzuò	工作
journey lǚxíng	旅行
jug guàn	罐
jumper tàoshān	套衫
junk *(boat)* fānchuán	帆船
just *(only)* jǐnjǐn	仅仅
just one jiù yīge	就一个
key yàoshi	钥匙
kilo gōngjīn	公斤
kilometre gōnglǐ	公里
kitchen chúfáng	厨房
knee xīgài	膝盖
knife dāo	刀
know: I don't know wǒ bù zhīdào	我不知道
Korea: North Korea Běi Cháoxiǎn	北朝鲜
South Korea Nán Cháoxiǎn	南朝鲜
ladies *(room)* nǚ cèsuǒ	女厕所
lady nǚshì	女士
lake hú	湖

lane xiǎoxiàng	小巷
Laos Lǎowō	老挝
large dà	大
last *(previous)* shàng yíge	上一个
(final) zuìhòu	最后
last year qùnián	去年
late *(at night)* wǎn	晚
(behind schedule) chí	迟
later yǐhòu	以后
left *(not right)* zuǒ	左
left luggage office xínglǐ jìcúnchù	行李寄存处
leg tuǐ	腿
lemon níngméng	柠檬
lemonade níngméng qìshuǐ	柠檬汽水
letter *(in mail)* xìn	信
letterbox xìnxiāng	信箱
lettuce wōjù	莴苣
library túshūguǎn	图书馆
life shēnghuó	生活
lift *(in hotel etc)* diàntī	电梯
could you give me a lift? nǐ néng bù néng ràng wǒ dāge chē?	你能不能让我搭个车？
light *(noun)* dēng	灯
have you got a light? jiè ge huǒ, xíng ma?	借个火，行吗？
(not heavy) qīng	轻
light bulb dēngpào	灯泡

lighter dáhuǒjī   打火机

like: I would like a ... wó   我想…
  xiǎng ...

  I like you wó xǐhuān nǐ   我喜欢你

  one like that xiàng nèige   象那个一样
  yíyàng

lipstick kǒuhóng   口红

litre shēng   升

little xiǎo   小

  just a little jiù yìdiǎndian   就一点点

liver gān   肝

lobster lóngxiā   龙虾

long cháng   长

  how long does it take? yào   要多长时间？
  duōcháng shíjiān?

lose: I've lost my ... wǒ ... diūle   我…丢了

lost property office shīwù   失物招领处
  zhāolǐng chù

lot: a lot xǔduō   许多

  a lot of money xǔ duō qián   许多钱

loud dàshēng de   大声的

love: I love you wǒ ài nǐ   我爱你

lovely (person) kě ài   可爱

  (thing) hén hǎo   很好

low dī   低

luck yùnqi   运气

  good luck! zhù nǐ hǎo yùn!   祝你好运！

luggage xínglǐ   行李

lunch wǔfàn 午饭

mail yóujiàn 邮件

make zuò 做

make-up huàzhuāngpǐn 化妆品

man nánrén 男人

manager jīnglǐ 经理

Mandarin Pǔtōnghuà 普通话

Mao Tse Tung jacket 中山装
  zhōngshānzhuāng

map dìtú 地图

market shìchǎng 市场

married: I'm married wǒ 我结婚了
  jiéhūnle

martial arts wǔshù 武术

matches huǒchái 火柴

material *(cloth)* bù 布

me wǒ 我
  it's for me zhè shì géi wǒde 这是给我的

medicine yào 药

meeting huì 会

melon guā 瓜

metre mǐ 米

midday: at midday zhōngwǔ 中午

middle: in the middle zài 在中间
  zhōngjiān

midnight: at midnight bànyè 半夜

mile yīnglǐ 英里

milk niúnǎi 牛奶

mine: it's mine shì wǒde   是我的

mineral water kuàngquánshuǐ   矿泉水

mirror jìngzi   镜子

Miss xiáojiě   小姐

mistake cuòwù   错误

money qián   钱

Mongolia Ménggǔ   蒙古

  Inner Mongolia Nèiměng   内蒙

  Outer Mongolia Wàiměng   外蒙

month yuè   月

moon yuèliàng   月亮

more gèng duō   更多

  more than bǐ ... duō   比…多

morning zǎoshàng   早上

mosquito wénzi   蚊子

mosquito net wénzhàng   蚊帐

mother māma   妈妈

motorbike mótuōchē   摩托车

mountain shān   山

moustache xiǎohúzi   小胡子

mouth zuǐba   嘴巴

Mr ... ... xiānsheng   …先生

Mrs ... ... fūren   …夫人

Ms ... ... nǚshì   …女士

much duō   多

  much better hǎo de duō   好得多

museum bówùguǎn   博物馆

mushrooms mógu   蘑菇

music yīnyuè	音乐
must: I must wǒ bìxū	我必须
my ... wǒde ...	我的…
narrow zhǎi	窄
near jìn	近
is it near here? lí zhèlǐ jìn ma?	离这里近吗？
necessary bìyào	必要
necklace xiàngliàn	项链
need: I need a ... wǒ xūyào ...	我需要…
needle zhēn	针
Nepal Níbóěr	尼泊尔
nephew zhízi	侄子
never cónglái bù	从来不
new xīn	新
news xīnwén	新闻
newspaper bàozhǐ	报纸
New Year Xīnnián	新年
happy New Year! Xīnniánhǎo	新年好
New Zealand Xīn Xīlán	新西兰
next xià yíge	下一个
next to ... zài ... pángbiān	在…旁边
nice (*person, weather*) hén hǎo	很好
(*meal*) hǎochī	好吃
(*town*) hén hǎo	很好
niece zhínǚ	侄女
night yè	夜
for one night yīyè	一夜
no bù *see page 10*	不

I've no money ... wǒ méi yǒu qián   我沒有钱

noisy hěnchǎo   很吵

north běi   北

nose bízi   鼻子

not bù   不

not for me wǒ bú yào   我不要

nothing méi yǒu shénme   沒有什么

now xiànzài   现在

number hàomǎ   号码

nurse hùshi   护士

of... ... de   …的

the name of the hotel lǚguǎnde míngzi   旅馆的名字

office bàngōngshì   办公室

often jīngcháng   经常

oil *(motor)* yóu   油

(vegetable) càiyóu   菜油

OK hǎo   好

old *(person)* lǎo   老

(things) jiù   旧

on zài ... shàngmian   在…上面

on the roof zài fángdǐng   在房顶

on the beach zài hǎitān   在海滩

one yī   一

that one nèi yíge   那一个

onion yángcōng   洋葱

only zhǐ yǒu   只有

open *(adj)* kāile	开了
opera gējù	歌剧
Peking Opera jīngjù	京剧
opposite: opposite the ... zài ... duìmiàn	在 … 对面
optician yǎnjìngdiàn	眼镜店
or huòzhe	或者
orange *(fruit)* gānjú	柑桔
(colour) júhuángsè	桔黄色
orange juice júzhī	桔汁
other: the other one lìng yígè	另一个
our(s) wǒmende	我们的
out: she's out tā bú zài	她不在
outside wàimian	外面
over: over there zài nàlǐ	在那里
oyster háo	蠔
packet *(of cigarettes etc)* bāo	包
paddy field dàotián	稻田
page yè	页
pagoda tǎ	塔
pair yìshuāng	一双
panda xióngmāo	熊猫
paper zhǐ	纸
parcel bāoguǒ	包裹
pardon? nǐ shuō shénme?	你说什么？
parents fùmǔ	父母
park *(noun)* gōngyuán	公园

(verb) tíngchē	停车
party *(celebration)* wǎnhuì	晚会
(group) tuántǐ	团体
pass *(mountain)* guānkǒu	关口
passport hùzhào	护照
path xiǎolù	小路
pavement rénxíngdào	人行道
pavilion tíngzi	亭子
pay fùqián	付钱
can I pay, please? wǒ kéyǐ fùqián ma?	我可以付钱吗？
peanuts huāshēng	花生
pen gāngbǐ	钢笔
pencil qiānbǐ	铅笔
penknife qiānbǐdāo	铅笔刀
people rén	人
pepper *(spice)* hújiāo	胡椒
(red/green) shìzijiāo	柿子椒
per: ... per cent bǎifēn zhī ...	百分之…
per night měi yè	每夜
perfume xiāngshuǐ	香水
perhaps kěnéng	可能
perm diàntàng	电烫
person rén	人
petrol qìyóu	汽油
petrol station jiāyóuzhàn	加油站
photograph *(noun)* zhàopiàn	照片
photograph *(verb)* zhàoxiàng	照相

photographer shèyǐngshī   摄影师
phrase book duìhuà shǒucè   对话手册
pickpocket páshǒu   扒手
picture túpiàn   图片
piece piàn   片
  a piece of ... yípiàn ...   一片…
pillow zhěntóu   枕头
pin biézhēn   别针
pineapple bōluó   菠萝
pink fěnhóng   粉红
pipe *(smoking)* yāndǒu   烟斗
  (water) guǎnzi   管子
place dìfāng   地方
plane fēijī   飞机
plant zhíwù   植物
plastic bag sùliàodài   塑料袋
plate pánzi   盘子
play *(in theatre)* huàjù   话剧
please: yes please kéyǐ, qǐng   可以，请
  could you please ...? nǐ   你能不能…？
  néng bù néng ...?
plug *(electric)* chātóu   插头
pocket kǒudài   口袋
poisonous yǒudú   有毒
police jǐngchá   警察
policeman jǐngchá   警察
polite yóu lǐmào   有礼貌
politics zhèngzhì   政治

pool shuǐchí		水池
poor *(not rich)* qióng		穷
pop music liúxíng yīnyuè		流行音乐
pork zhūròu		猪肉
porter *(hotel)* ménfáng		门房
(station etc) bānyùn gōngrén		搬运工人
possible kěnéng		可能
post *(mail)* yóujiàn		邮件
postcard míngxìnpiàn		明信片
poster zhāotiē		招贴
post office yóujú		邮局
potato tǔdòu		土豆
pound *(money)* yīngbàng		英镑
prawn duìxiā		对虾
pregnant huáiyùn		怀孕
present *(gift)* lǐwù		礼物
pretty piàoliang		漂亮
price jiàgé		价格
problem wèntí		问题
pronounce fāyīn		发音
pull lā		拉
puncture chuānkǒng		穿孔
purse qiánbāo		钱包
push tuī		推
pyjamas shuìyī		睡衣
question wèntí		问题
queue *(noun)* duì		队
quick kuài		快

quiet *(place, hotel etc)* ānjìng   安静

quite: quite a lot xiāng dāng   相当多
  duō

radiator sànrèqì   散热器

radio shōuyīnjī   收音机

railway tiělù   铁路

rain yǔ   雨

  it's raining xiàyǔ le   下雨了

rat láoshǔ   老鼠

razor tìdāo   剃刀

razor blades tìhú dāopiàn   剃胡刀片

read dú   读

ready zhǔnbèi hǎo   准备好

receipt shōujù   收据

record *(music)* chàngpiàn   唱片

red hóngsè   红色

religion zōngjiào   宗教

rent *(for room etc)* fángzū   房租

  (verb) zū   租

repair *(verb)* xiūlǐ   修理

reserve yùdìng   预订

restaurant fàndiàn   饭店

return *(come back)* fǎnhuí   返回

  (give back) huán   还

rice *(cooked)* mǐfàn   米饭

  (uncooked) mǐ   米

rice bowl fànwǎn   饭碗

rice field dàotián   稻田

rich *(person)* hén yǒuqián — 很有钱

right *(not left)* yòu — 右

  (correct) duì — 对

ring *(on finger)* jièzhi — 戒指

river hé — 河

road lù — 路

roof fángdǐng — 房顶

room *(hotel)* fángjiān — 房间

  (space) kōngjiān — 空间

rope shéngzi — 绳子

round *(adj)* yuánde — 圆的

rubber *(material)* xiàngjiāo — 橡胶

  (eraser) xiàngpí — 橡皮

rubbish *(waste)* lājī — 垃圾

  (poor quality) tài zāogāo le — 太糟糕了

rucksack bèibāo — 背包

ruins fèixū — 废墟

run pǎo — 跑

Russia Éguó — 俄国

sad shāngxīn — 伤心

safe *(not in danger)* píng ān — 平安

  (not dangerous) ānquán — 安全

safety pin biézhēn — 别针

salad sèlā — 色拉

salt yán — 盐

same yíyàng — 一样

  the same again please zài lái yíge — 再来一个

sand shā	沙
sandals liángxié	凉鞋
sandwich sānmíngzhì	三明治
sanitary towels wèishēngjīn	卫生巾
sauce jiàng	酱
sausage xiāngcháng	香肠
say: how do you say in	…用汉语怎么说？
Chinese …? … yòng Hànyǔ	
zěnme shuō?	
school xuéxiào	学校
scissors jiǎndāo	剪刀
Scotland Sūgélán	苏格兰
screwdriver luósīdāo	螺丝刀
sea hǎi	海
seafood hǎiwèi	海味
seat zuòwèi	座位
seatbelt ānquándài	安全带
second *(in series)* dì èr	第二
(of time) miǎo	秒
see kànjian	看见
I see! wǒ míngbai le!	我明白了！
sell mài	卖
sellotape *(R)* tòumíng jiāodài	透明胶带
separately *(pay)* fēn kāi fù	分开付
sesame oil máyóu	麻油
shade: in the shade zài	在荫凉处
yīnliáng chù	
shampoo xǐfàjīng	洗发精

shave guāhúzi	刮胡子
shaving foam guā hú pàomò	刮胡泡沫
she tā	她
sheet *(for bed)* chuángdān	床单
ship chuán	船
shirt chènshān	衬衫
shoe laces xiédài	鞋带
shoes xié	鞋
shop shāngdiàn	商店
short *(person)* ǎi	矮
(time) duǎn	短
shorts duǎnkù	短裤
shoulder jiānbǎng	肩膀
shower *(in bathroom)* línyù	淋浴
shrimps xiā	虾
shut guān	关
shutter chuāngbǎn	窗板
Siberia Xībólìyà	西伯利亚
side street xiǎojiē	小街
sight *(view)* fēngjǐng	风景
silk sīchóu	丝绸
Silk Road sīchóu zhī lù	丝绸之路
silver yín	银
sing chànggē	唱歌
Singapore Xīnjiāpō	新加坡
single: I'm single wǒ shì dānshēn	我是单身
sister jiěmèi	姐妹
sit down zuòxià	坐下

skirt qúnzi	裙子
sky tiān kōng	天空
sleep shuìjiào	睡觉
slow(ly) màn	慢
small xiǎo	小
smell *(have bad smell)* nánwénde qìwèi	难闻的气味
smile *(verb)* xiào	笑
smoke *(noun)* yān	烟
do you smoke? nǐ xīyān ma?	你吸烟吗？
snake shé	蛇
so: so good zhēnhǎo	真好
not so much búyào nàme duō	不要那么多
soap féizào	肥皂
socks wàzi	袜子
soft *(material etc)* ruǎn	软
soft drink ruǎn yǐnliào	软饮料
sole *(of shoes)* xiédǐ	鞋底
somebody yǒurén	有人
something yǒuxiē dōngxi	有些东西
sometimes yǒu shí	有时
somewhere mǒuchù	某处
son érzi	儿子
song gē	歌
soon bù jiǔ	不久
sorry duìbuqǐ	对不起
sorry? nǐ shuō shénme?	你说什么？
soup tāng	汤

south nán		南
souvenir jìniànpǐn		纪念品
soy sauce jiàngyóu		酱油
spanner huó bānshǒu		活扳手
speak jiǎng		讲
spider zhīzhū		蜘蛛
spoon sháozi		勺子
spring *(season)* chūntiān		春天
spring onion xiǎocōng		小葱
stairs lóutī		楼梯
stamp *(for letter)* yóupiào		邮票
start *(noun)* kāishǐ		开始
station *(railway)* huǒchē zhàn		火车站
steak niúpái		牛排
steal: my bag has been stolen wǒde bāo bèi tōule		我的包被偷了
sticky rice nuòmǐ		糯米
stockings chángtǒngwà		长筒袜
stomach wèi		胃
stop *(bus stop)* chēzhàn		车站
stop here tíng zhèlǐ		停这里
storm bàofēngyǔ		暴风雨
straight: it's straight ahead yìzhí cháoqián		一直朝前
street jiē		街
string xìshéng		细绳
student xuéshēng		学生

stupid	yúchǔn	愚蠢
sugar	táng	糖
suit *(noun)*	xīzhuāng	西装
suitcase	shǒutíxiāng	手提箱
sun	tàiyáng	太阳
sunblock *(cream)*	fángshàirǔ	防晒乳
sunburnt	shàihēide	晒黑的
sunglasses	tàiyángjìng	太阳镜
sunshade	yángsǎn	阳伞
sunstroke	zhòngshǔ	中暑
suntan lotion	fángshàijì	防晒剂
supermarket	chāojí shìchǎng	超级市场
sure: I'm sure	wǒ quèxìn	我确信
are you sure?	nǐ néng kěndìng ma?	你能肯定吗？
surname	xìng	姓
sweat *(noun)*	hàn	汗
(verb)	chūhàn	出汗
sweet *(confectionery)*	táng	糖
(to taste)	tián	甜
sweet and sour	tángcù	糖醋
sweltering: it's sweltering	mēnrè	闷热
swim *(verb)*	yóuyǒng	游泳
swimming costume	yóuyǒngyī	游泳衣
swimming pool	yóuyǒngchí	游泳池
swimming trunks	yóuyǒngkù	游泳裤
table	zhuōzi	桌子
table tennis	pīngpāngqiú	乒乓球

Taiwan Táiwān	台湾
take (*someone somewhere*) dàilǐng	带领
(*something somewhere*) dài	带
talk (*verb*) shuōhuà	说话
tall gāo	高
tampons miánsāi	棉塞
Taoism Dàojiào	道教
tap shuǐlóngtóu	水龙头
tape (*cassette*) cídài	磁带
taxi chūzūchē	出租车
tea chá	茶
telegram diànbào	电报
telephone diànhuà	电话
television diànshì	电视
temperature (*weather*) qìwēn	气温
(*fever*) rèdù	热度
temple miào	庙
tent zhàngpéng	帐篷
Terra Cotta Army Bīngmáyǒng	兵马佣
terrible zhēn zāogāo	眞糟糕
Thailand Tàiguó	泰国
than bǐ ... gèng ...	比…更…
smaller than bǐ ... xiǎo	比…小
thank you xièxie	谢谢
that: that woman nèige nǚrén	那个女人
that man nèige nánrén	那个男人
what's that nà shì shénme?	那是什么？
theatre jùyuàn	剧院

their(s)	tāmende	他们的
them	tāmen	他们
then *(after that)*	ránhòu	然后
(at that time)	nà shí	那时
there	nàlǐ	那里
there is/are	yǒu ...	有…
is/are there ...?	yǒu ... ma?	有…吗？
there isn't/aren't ...	méi yǒu ...	沒有…
thermos flask	rèshuǐpíng	热水瓶
these	zhèxiē	这些
they	tāmen	他们
thick	hòu	厚
thin *(thing)*	báo	薄
(person)	shòu	瘦
thing	dōngxi	东西
think	xiǎng	想
thirsty: I'm thirsty	wǒ kóukě	我口渴
this: this street	zhè tiáo jiē	这条街
this one	zhège	这个
what's this?	zhè shì shénme?	这是什么？
those	nàxiē	那些
throat	hóulóng	喉咙
through	jīngguò	经过
thunderstorm	léiyǔ	雷雨
Tibet	Xīzàng	西藏
ticket	piào	票
tie *(around neck)*	lǐngdài	领带
tights	liánkùwà	连裤袜

time shíjiān		时间
next time xià cì		下次
what time is it? jídiǎn le?		几点了？
timetable shíjiānbiǎo		时间表
tin *(can)* guàntou		罐头
tin opener guàntou qǐzi		罐头起子
tip *(money)* xiǎofèi		小费
tired lèi		累
tissues báozhǐ		薄纸
to dào		到
to England qù Yīnggélán		去英格兰
toast *(bread)* kǎo miànbāopiàn		烤面包片
today jīntiān		今天
together yìqǐ		一起
toilet cèsuǒ		厕所
toilet paper shóuzhǐ		手纸
tomato xīhóngshì		西红柿
tomorrow míngtiān		明天
tonic *(water)* kuàngquánshuǐ		矿泉水
tonight jīntian wǎnshang		今天晚上
too *(also)* yě		也
(excessively) tài		太
tooth yá		牙
toothbrush yáshuā		牙刷
toothpaste yágāo		牙膏
tour *(noun)* lǚxíng		旅行
tourist lǚxíngzhě		旅行者
tourist office lǚxíng shè		旅行社

towel máojīn	毛巾
town chéngzhèn	城镇
traditional chuántǒng	传统
traffic lights hónglǜ dēng	红绿灯
train huǒchē	火车
translate fānyì	翻译
travel agent lǚxíngshè	旅行社
traveller's cheque lǚxíng zhīpiào	旅行支票
tree shù	树
trousers cháng kù	长裤
true zhēnde	眞的
trunk *(US: car)* xínglixiāng	行李箱
try *(try out, test)* shì shi	试试
T-shirt duǎnxiù yuánlǐng hànshān	短袖圆领汗衫
tweezers nièzi	镊子
tyre lúntāi	轮胎
umbrella yúsǎn	雨伞
uncle shūshu	叔叔
under zài ... xiàmiàn	在…下面
United States Měiguó	美国
vaccination yùfángjiēzhòng	预防接种
vanilla xiāngcǎo	香草
vase huāpíng	花瓶
vegetables shūcài	蔬菜
vegetarian chīsù de	吃素的
very fēicháng	非常
Vietnam Yuènán	越南
village cūnzhuāng	村庄

visa qiānzhèng	签证
visit *(place)* cānguān	参观
(people) bàifǎng	拜访
voice shēngyīn	声音
voltage diànyā	电压
wait děng	等
waiter zhāodài	招待
waitress nǚzhāodài	女招待
Wales Wēi'ěrshì	威尔士
wall qiáng	墙
the Great Wall of China Chángchéng	长城
wallet qiánbāo	钱包
warm nuǎnhuo	暖和
washing powder xǐyīfěn	洗衣粉
wasp huángfēng	黄蜂
watch *(wrist)* shóubiǎo	手表
(verb) kàn	看
water shuǐ	水
we wǒmen	我们
weather tiānqì	天气
wedding hūnlǐ	婚礼
week xīngqī	星期
welcome: you're welcome bú kèqi	不客气
west xī	西
Western-style xīshì	西式
wet shī	湿

what? shénme?	什么？
wheel lúnzi	轮子
when? shénme shíhòu?	什么时候？
where? nálǐ?	哪里？
where is ...? ... zài nálǐ?	…在哪里？
which: which one? nǎ yíge?	哪一个？
whiskey wēishìjì	威士忌
white báisè	白色
who? shúi?	谁？
why? wèishenme?	为什么？
wide kuān	宽
wife qīzi	妻子
wind fēng	风
window chuāng	窗
wine jiǔ	酒
with hé ... yìqǐ	和…一起
without méiyǒu	沒有
woman fùnǚ	妇女
wood mùtou	木头
wool yángmáo	羊毛
word cí	词
work (noun) gōngzuò	工作
(verb) gōngzuò	工作
it's not working huàile	坏了
write xiě	写
could you write it down?	你能不能写一下？
nǐ néng bù néng xiě yíxia?	
wrong cuò	错

Yangtze Gorges Chángjiāng sānxiá	长江三峡
Yangtze River Chángjiāng	长江
year nián	年
yellow huángsè	黄色
Yellow River Huánghé	黄河
Yellow Sea Huánghǎi	黄海
yes shìde	是的
yesterday zuótiān	昨天
yet: not yet hái méine	还没呢
yoghurt suānnǎi	酸奶
you nǐ	你
(plural) nǐmen	你们
young niánqīng	年轻的
your(s) nǐde	你的
(plural) nǐmen	你们的
zip lāliàn	拉链
zoo dòngwùyuán	动物园